Index

1. Introduction

1.1 World record concept

The concept of a "world record" has fascinated humanity for centuries, fueling our desire to overcome limits and achieve extraordinary goals. But what does it really mean to hold a world record? In simple terms, a record represents an absolute first in a certain activity or category, which is officially recognized as the best, the biggest, the fastest, or simply the most extraordinary.

The Guinness World Record is the best-known keeper of these records. Founded in 1955, its purpose is to document and certify exceptional, often incredible, feats from every corner of the globe. Records can be achieved in any area: from the physical and intellectual capabilities of human beings, to the wonders of the natural world, to technological innovations and artistic expressions.

Each record tells a unique story of dedication, passion and, sometimes, eccentricity. Behind every record there is an individual, a group or a community who has chosen to pursue something extraordinary, pushing themselves beyond their limits.

Criteria for a world record

Not everything, however, can be considered a record. To be officially recognized, a record must meet specific criteria, including:

- **Measurability:** The record must be quantifiable and objectively measurable (e.g. time, size, number of repetitions).
- **Universality:** It must be replicable by anyone in the world, under equal conditions.
- **Uniqueness:** It must not overlap with other existing records.
- **Documented evidence:** It must be accompanied by verifiable evidence, such as videos, photos and testimonials.

This introductory section is an invitation to explore the wonderful world of records and immerse yourself in incredible stories that celebrate creativity, determination and the human spirit. Which record will surprise you the most?

1.2 The rules of the Guinness World Record

For a feat to be recognized as an official record by Guinness World Records, a series of strict rules must be met. These rules serve to ensure that each record is verifiable, fair and represents a unique record. Let's look at the fundamental principles that govern the approval and certification of records.

1.2.1 Fundamental requirements

1. **Measurability**
   Each record must be able to be precisely measured using standardized units of measurement, such as time, length, weight or quantity. For example, you cannot certify a record based on personal impressions or subjective judgments.
2. **Universality**
   A record must be replicable anywhere in the world by anyone with the same skills or tools. For example, a record that requires a unique environmental condition, such as a specific altitude, may be excluded.
3. **Uniqueness**
   The proposed record must represent an exclusive record. There cannot be two similar records that risk overlapping. For example, "Highest jump on one leg" is acceptable, but "Highest jump on one right leg" may not be approved because it is too specific.
4. **Ethics   and   safety**
   No record must endanger the life or health of people, animals or the environment. Records that include dangerous or illegal activities are automatically excluded.
5. **Documented   evidence**
   The application must include complete and verifiable evidence, such as:
   - Full video recordings.
   - High resolution photographs.
   - Official testimonies from judges, experts or notaries.

1.2.2 Approval procedure

1. **Record**   **proposal**
   Anyone can propose a record by filling out a form on the official Guinness World Record website. The proposal must include a detailed description of the undertaking and how it will be executed and measured.

2. **Preliminary**   **evaluation**
   Guinness World Record experts review the proposal to ensure that it meets key criteria and is unique and replicable.

3. **Official**   **attempt**
   Once the proposal is approved, the undertaking must be executed following the guidelines provided. An official Guinness judge is often required to certify the attempt.

4. **Final**   **inspection**   **and**   **certification**
   After the attempt, the collected evidence is sent to Guinness World Records for further review. If everything complies, the record is certified and placed in the official archive.

1.2.3 Most popular categories

- **Physical:** Speed, strength, endurance.
- **Intellectuals:** Memory, logical skills.
- **Artistic:** Larger or more complex works.
- **Technological:** Unique innovations and inventions.
- **Curiosity:** Extraordinary collections or unusual feats.

1.2.4 Curious aspects

- Thousands of applications are received every year, but only a small percentage are accepted.
- Some existing records are so specific that they remain unbeaten for decades.
- You can request that your attempt be judged directly by a Guinness representative, but this incurs additional costs.

These rules ensure that every record is authentic, verifiable and worthy of inclusion in the Guinness World Record. Following these guidelines is essential for anyone who dreams of making their mark in world record history!

1.3 Invitation to discover the types of records

The world of records is incredibly diverse, full of surprises and extraordinary stories. Each page of the "Book of Records 2025" is a journey through the infinite possibilities of the human being, nature and technological wonders. This invitation to discovery will guide you through the types of records in the book, with a map of the incredible feats you will find.

1.3.1 What does it mean to explore a record?

Each record contains a challenge, a dream or a unique curiosity. It ranges from the impressive speed of the cheetah to the incredible abilities of a person who can memorize thousands of numbers in just a few minutes. Exploring a record isn't just about discovering the "best" in something, it's about immersing yourself in stories that celebrate diversity, creativity, and determination.

1.3.2 The major categories of the book

This book is structured into sections that represent the main thematic areas of world records:

1. **Natural World**
   o Discover the extraordinary abilities of animals and plants and the most extreme phenomena of nature.
2. **Human being**
   o Celebrate the exceptional physical feats, artistic talents and curious records of people from all over the world.
3. **Science and Technology**

     o Immerse yourself in scientific and technological advances that continue to push the boundaries of what is possible.

4. **Art and Culture**
   - o From cinema to literature, discover the masterpieces that have marked history.
5. **Sport**
   - o Experience the thrills of unique athletic feats that test the limits of the human body.
6. **Curiosities and Collections**
   - o Explore the most unusual records and bizarre collections that have fascinated the world.
7. **Youth and Kids' Zone**
   - o Discover the talent of the new generation of record holders, with stories that inspire little ones.
8. **Travel and Explorations**
   - o Embark on an adventure among the most remote places and the most incredible environments on the planet.
9. **Flashback e Poster**
   - o Dive into the history of records to discover how they have changed over time.

1.3.3 How to read the book

Each chapter is divided into sections and subsections, so as to guide you in discovering records that range from the most serious undertakings to the funniest curiosities. You can follow the proposed order or skip to the sections that interest you most.

Each record is accompanied by a detailed description, images and curiosities that make it unique. Some records are told through incredible stories, while others will leave you speechless with the numbers they represent.

1.3.4 A personal invitation

Let yourself be inspired by the extraordinary feats recounted in these pages. This book is not just a collection of records, but a celebration of what makes humanity and the natural world so special. Who knows? Perhaps by reading these pages you will find your inspiration to attempt a record of your own.

The "2025 Book of Records" is a window into what makes our world unique. Prepare to be amazed, entertained and, above all, inspired. What will be your favorite record? The journey begins here!

2. Natural World

2.1 Animals (Introduction)

Animals are the protagonists of some of the most extraordinary records on our planet. From the power of a lion's roar to the lightning speed of the cheetah, the animal kingdom never ceases to amaze us. Each species has unique characteristics that make it perfect for tackling specific challenges, whether it be survival, adaptation or pure spectacularity.

2.1.1 Mammals

Mammals are one of the most fascinating classes of the animal kingdom, celebrated for their diversity and adaptability. This subsection explores the 20 most extraordinary records from the mammal world.

---

1. The largest mammal: the blue whale

- **Details:** With a length of up to 30 meters and a weight of over 150 tonnes, the blue whale holds the record for the largest mammal to ever exist.
- **Habitat:** Oceans around the world.

- **Curiosity:** His tongue weighs as much as an elephant and his heart as heavy as a compact car.

---

2. The fastest mammal: the cheetah

- **Details:** Capable of reaching a speed of 112 km/h, the cheetah is the fastest land mammal.
- **Habitat:** Savannas and prairies of Africa.
- **Curiosity:** It can accelerate from 0 to 100 km/h in just 3 seconds, faster than many sports cars.

---

3. The longest-lived mammal: the Greenland whale

- **Details:** With a life expectancy exceeding 200 years, this whale is the longest-lived mammal.
- **Habitat:** Arctic and subarctic waters.
- **Curiosity:** Some specimens still have harpoons dating back to the 19th century embedded in their bodies.

---

4. The smallest mammal: the bumblebee bat

- **Details:** This tiny bat weighs just 2 grams and is only 3 cm long.
- **Habitat:** Limestone caves of Thailand and Myanmar.
- **Curiosity:** Despite its size, it hunts insects with incredible precision.

---

5. The mammal with the longest jump: the red kangaroo

- **Details:** It can jump up to 13.5 meters in a single bound.
- **Habitat:** Arid and semi-arid areas of Australia.
- **Curiosity:** Its tail acts as a balance when jumping.

---

6. The strongest mammal: the African elephant

- **Details:** It can lift objects weighing up to 9 tons with its trunk.
- **Habitat:** Savannas, forests and wooded areas of Africa.
- **Curiosity:** The proboscis is made up of approximately 40,000 muscles.

---

7. The mammal with the greatest resistance to poison: the honey badger

- **Details:** It is immune to the venom of deadly snakes and other predators.
- **Habitat:** Africa, the Middle East and South Asia.
- **Curiosity:** His fame is so legendary that he has been credited with "fearless" behavior in documentaries.

---

8. The tallest mammal: the giraffe

- **Details:** It can reach a height of 6 meters, thanks to its neck up to 2.5 meters long.
- **Habitat:** African savannas.
- **Curiosity:** His heart is powerful enough to pump blood up to his head, fighting gravity.

---

9. The fastest marine mammal: the killer whale

- **Details:** It can swim up to 56 km/h.
- **Habitat:** Oceans around the world.
- **Curiosity:** It is a social predator that hunts in highly organized groups.

---

10. The mammal with the longest sleep: the brown bat

- **Details:** He can sleep up to 20 hours a day.

10

- **Habitat:** Forests, caves and urban areas of North America.
- **Curiosity:** This long rest helps conserve energy during hibernation.

---

11. The mammal with the most teeth: the South American river dolphin

- **Details:** It can have up to 252 teeth.
- **Habitat:** Amazonian rivers and their tributaries.
- **Curiosity:** It uses its teeth not only for eating, but also for grasping objects.

---

12. The heaviest mammal: the African elephant

- **Details:** It can weigh up to 7,000 kg.
- **Habitat:** Forested areas and African savannas.
- **Curiosity:** Despite his weight, he is a surprisingly skilled swimmer.

---

13. The mammal with the best hearing: the bat

- **Details:** It uses echolocation to orient itself and hunt.
- **Habitat:** Widespread throughout the world, except in the polar regions.
- **Curiosity:** It can perceive sounds up to a frequency of 120 kHz.

---

14. The most territorial mammal: the gray wolf

- **Details:** It protects its territory, which can extend up to 2,500 km^2.
- **Habitat:** Forests, tundras and grasslands of Eurasia and North America.

- **Curiosity:** It communicates with howls that can be heard up to 16 km away.

---

15. The most affectionate mammal: the bonobo

- **Details:** It is known for extremely close and peaceful social bonds.
- **Habitat:** Rainforests of the Democratic Republic of the Congo.
- **Curiosity:** It shares 98.7% of its DNA with humans.

---

16. The mammal with the longest tail: the giant pangolin

- **Details:** Its tail can be longer than the body, reaching up to 60 cm.
- **Habitat:** Forests and savannahs of Africa.
- **Curiosity:** The tail is used for climbing and as a support.

---

17. The mammal with the largest lung capacity: the sperm whale

- **Details:** He can hold his breath for over 90 minutes.
- **Habitat:** Deep oceans around the world.
- **Curiosity:** It is the natural predator of giant squid.

---

18. The mammal with the greatest ability to jump heights: the puma

- **Details:** It can jump up to 5.5 meters vertically.
- **Habitat:** Mountains and forests of the American continent.
- **Curiosity:** Use this ability to hunt prey in trees.

---

19. The mammal with the thickest fur: the sea otter

- **Details:** It has up to 1 million hair follicles per square centimeter.
- **Habitat:** North Pacific Ocean.
- **Curiosity:** It has no layers of fat, so it depends on its thick fur to maintain heat.

---

20. The most migratory mammal: the gray whale

- **Details:** It migrates over 20,000 km per year between feeding and breeding areas.
- **Habitat:** North Pacific and Arctic Oceans.
- **Curiosity:** This migration is one of the longest in the animal kingdom.

This selection demonstrates how the world of mammals is full of surprises. Which record surprised you the most?

2.1.2 Birds

Birds are among the most extraordinary creatures on the planet, known for their ability to fly, their bright colors and their incredible abilities. Each species seems to challenge the laws of nature with feats that make them protagonists of surprising records. Here are 20 amazing records held by birds.

---

1. The fastest flying bird: the peregrine falcon

- **Details:** During its hunting dives, the peregrine falcon can reach speeds of over 389 km/h, making it the fastest animal on the planet.
- **Habitat:** Widespread throughout the world, except in the polar regions.

- **Curiosity:** Its vision is so acute that it can spot prey from over 3 kilometers away.

---

2. The bird with the largest wingspan: the howling albatross

- **Details:** With a wingspan that can reach 3.7 meters, the howling albatross holds this record.
- **Habitat:** Oceans of the Southern Hemisphere.
- **Curiosity:** It can fly for days without ever landing, covering thousands of kilometers.

---

3. The smallest bird: the bee hummingbird

- **Details:** This tiny bird weighs just 2 grams and measures approximately 5 cm.
- **Habitat:** Cuba and nearby islands.
- **Curiosity:** It can flap its wings up to 80 times per second, allowing it to soar through the air.

---

4. The heaviest bird: the ostrich

- **Details:** With a weight that can exceed 150 kg, the ostrich is the heaviest bird in the world.
- **Habitat:** African savannahs and deserts.
- **Curiosity:** Although it cannot fly, it can run up to 70 km/h.

---

5. The bird with the longest flight: the bar-tailed godwit

- **Details:** This tireless migrant can fly non-stop for over 12,000 kilometers.
- **Habitat:** From Alaska to New Zealand during migration.
- **Curiosity:** It can lose up to 50% of its body weight during travel.

14

6. The bird with the loudest song: the white bellbird

- **Details:** Its call can reach 125 decibels, equivalent to the sound of a jet taking off.
- **Habitat:** Tropical forests of South America.
- **Curiosity:** He uses his song to attract females, but must do so from a distance so as not to damage their hearing.

7. The bird with the highest flight altitude: the Indian goose

- **Details:** It can fly over the Himalayas, reaching altitudes above 9,000 metres.
- **Habitat:** Central and South Asia.
- **Curiosity:** It has a unique respiratory system that allows it to survive in oxygen-limited conditions.

8. The longest-lived bird: Laysan albatross

- **Details:** A specimen called "Wisdom" is over 70 years old and is still able to reproduce.
- **Habitat:** North Pacific Ocean.
- **Curiosity:** He has traveled millions of kilometers during his life.

9. The most colorful bird: the Indian peacock

- **Details:** Its iridescent plumage is unique in the animal kingdom, with colors ranging from blue to green.
- **Habitat:** Tropical forests of southern Asia.
- **Curiosity:** Males use their tails to impress females during courtship.

10. The bird with the largest nest: the bald eagle

- **Details:** Bald eagle nests can weigh more than a ton and measure up to 10 feet in diameter.
- **Habitat:** Nord America.
- **Curiosity:** It can take a couple years to build and perfect their nest.

---

11. The bird with the most waterproof plumage: the emperor penguin

- **Details:** The penguin's plumage is extremely dense and oily, allowing it to survive in the frigid waters of Antarctica.
- **Habitat:** Antarctica.
- **Curiosity:** During the winter, males protect the eggs by keeping them warm between their paws.

---

12. The bird with the greatest intelligence: the common raven

- **Details:** He is capable of using tools, solving complex problems and remembering human faces.
- **Habitat:** Temperate regions of the Northern Hemisphere.
- **Curiosity:** Crows can imitate sounds, including human voices.

---

13. The smallest migratory bird: the ruby-throated hummingbird

- **Details:** This tiny bird migrates over 3,000 kilometers each year.
- **Habitat:** North and Central America.
- **Curiosity:** During migration it can cross the Gulf of Mexico without stopping.

---

14. The fastest bird on the ground: the emu

- **Details:** It can run up to 50 km/h.
- **Habitat:** Desert and semi-desert areas of Australia.
- **Curiosity:** It has three toes that provide excellent traction on sandy ground.

---

15. The bird with the bill longer than the body: the roseate spoonbill

- **Details:** Its beak can be as long as its body.
- **Habitat:** Swamps and wetlands of the American continent.
- **Curiosity:** It uses its beak to filter small fish and insects from the water.

---

16. The loudest bird: the kakapo

- **Details:** During the mating season, kakapo calls can be heard up to 5 km away.
- **Habitat:** New Zealand.
- **Curiosity:** It is one of the rarest birds in the world, with a population of only 250 individuals.

---

17. The bird with the most feathers: the mute swan

- **Details:** It can have up to 25,000 feathers on its body.
- **Habitat:** Lakes, rivers and swamps of the Northern Hemisphere.
- **Curiosity:** Their beauty has made them symbols of elegance in many cultures.

---

18. The largest bird in height: the ostrich

- **Details:** It can reach a height of 2.7 meters.
- **Habitat:** African savannas.

- **Curiosity:** Its eggs are the largest in the animal kingdom, weighing about 1.4 kg.

---

19. The bird with the smallest eggs: the bee hummingbird

- **Details:** Its eggs weigh only 0.5 grams.
- **Habitat:** Cuba.
- **Curiosity:** The eggs hatch after just two weeks of incubation.

---

20. The bird that flies the furthest every day: the swallow

- **Details:** It can cover over 800 km in a single day during migration.
- **Habitat:** Spread all over the world.
- **Curiosity:** Swallows feed in flight, catching insects at high speeds.

Birds show us that the sky is not the limit, but an opportunity for exploration and conquest. Which of these records is your favorite?

2.1.3 Reptiles and Amphibians

Reptiles and amphibians are extraordinary creatures that have populated our planet for millions of years, often holding unique records thanks to their physiological and behavioral characteristics. Here is a list of 20 extraordinary records belonging to these two fascinating groups.

---

1. The largest reptile: the saltwater crocodile

- **Details:** It can reach a length of 7 meters and a weight of more than 1,000 kg.
- **Habitat:** Estuaries, rivers and coasts of South Asia and Australia.
- **Curiosity:** It is one of the most dangerous predators for humans, but mainly hunts fish and mammals.

2. The fastest reptile: the basilisk lizard

- **Details:** It can run up to 12 km/h on land and 5 km/h on water.
- **Habitat:** Rainforests of Central and South America.
- **Curiosity:** It is called the "Jesus Christ lizard" because of its ability to walk on water.

3. The most poisonous reptile: the inland taipan

- **Details:** The venom of this snake is lethal and can kill a human in less than an hour.
- **Habitat:** Arid plains of central Australia.
- **Curiosity:** Despite its dangerousness, it is extremely shy and rarely attacks humans.

4. The longest-lived reptile: the Seychelles giant tortoise

- **Details:** It can live over 190 years.
- **Habitat:** Isole Seychelles.
- **Curiosity:** Jonathan, a giant tortoise, is the oldest recorded reptile, at over 190 years old.

5. The smallest reptile: the dwarf chameleon

- **Details:** This chameleon measures just 2.9 cm.
- **Habitat:** Forests of Madagascar.

- **Curiosity:** Despite its tiny size, it is a skilled insect hunter.

---

6. The longest snake: the reticulated python

- **Details:** It can exceed 10 meters in length.
- **Habitat:** Rainforests and swamps of Southeast Asia.
- **Curiosity:** It is capable of swallowing prey as large as deer thanks to its flexible jaw.

---

7. The largest amphibian: the Chinese giant salamander

- **Details:** It can reach a length of 1.8 meters.
- **Habitat:** Mountain rivers and streams of China.
- **Curiosity:** It is considered a living fossil, having existed almost unchanged for millions of years.

---

8. The most poisonous amphibian: the golden dart frog

- **Details:** Its venom can kill up to 20 people.
- **Habitat:** Rainforests of Central and South America.
- **Curiosity:** The poison is used by local populations to dip hunting arrows.

---

9. The reptile with the most powerful bite: the Nile crocodile

- **Details:** Its bite can exert a force of over 2,200 kg/cm².
- **Habitat:** Rivers and lakes of sub-Saharan Africa.
- **Curiosity:** It is known for its spinning technique to dismember prey.

---

10. The reptile with the best camouflage: the panther chameleon

- **Details:** It can change color in seconds, adapting to its surroundings.
- **Habitat:** Forests of Madagascar.
- **Curiosity:** The color change also serves to communicate and regulate body temperature.

11. The reptile with the longest tail: the giant lizard

- **Details:** Its tail can be twice the length of the body.
- **Habitat:** Tropical forests of Southeast Asia.
- **Curiosity:** It uses its tail to defend itself from predators.

12. The fastest snake: the black mamba

- **Details:** It can move up to 20 km/h.
- **Habitat:** Savannas and forests of sub-Saharan Africa.
- **Curiosity:** It is one of the most feared snakes in the world due to its speed and poisonousness.

13. The most resistant reptile: the tokay gecko

- **Details:** It can survive without food for weeks and regenerate body parts, such as its tail.
- **Habitat:** Southeast Asian.
- **Curiosity:** Its characteristic call seems to say "tokay", from which it takes its name.

14. The loudest amphibian: the American bullfrog

- **Details:** Its call can be heard over 1 km away.
- **Habitat:** Wetlands of North America.
- **Curiosity:** Males use calls to defend their territory.

15. The oldest reptile: the hawksbill turtle

- **Details:** This species has existed for over 100 million years.
- **Habitat:** Tropical oceans.
- **Curiosity:** Its scales have historically been used to create ornaments.

---

16. The most invasive reptile: the green anaconda

- **Details:** It is one of the most invasive species, capable of adapting to different habitats.
- **Habitat:** South American rainforests.
- **Curiosity:** It can reach 250 kg in weight.

---

17. The most toxic amphibian: the poison dart frog

- **Details:** Each gram of its venom can kill hundreds of animals.
- **Habitat:** Central American rainforests.
- **Curiosity:** Its bright color warns predators of its toxicity.

---

18. The longest reptile that ever lived: the Titanoboa

- **Details:** This prehistoric snake could reach 13 meters in length.
- **Habitat:** Tropical forests of the Paleocene period.
- **Curiosity:** It was so big that it could hunt crocodiles.

---

19. The reptile with the toughest skin: the three-banded armadillo

- **Details:** Its armor is so resistant that it can withstand the attack of a predator.
- **Habitat:** Sud America.
- **Curiosity:** It can roll up completely for protection.

20. The amphibian with the most permeable skin: the fire salamander

- **Details:** It can absorb water directly through the skin.
- **Habitat:** Moist forests of Europe.
- **Curiosity:** Its skin is a biological indicator of environmental quality.

These records highlight the incredible abilities and adaptability of reptiles and amphibians. Which of these firsts impressed you the most?

2.1.4 Insects

Insects are the largest and most diverse group of animals on the planet, and among their ranks are some of the most extraordinary creatures in terms of skill, strength, speed and adaptability. Here is a collection of 20 incredible records held by insects.

1. The fastest flying insect: the Australian dragonfly

- **Details:** It can reach speeds of 97 km/h, making it the fastest flying insect in the world.
- **Habitat:** Wetlands and lakes in Australia.
- **Curiosity:** Its wings work independently, allowing for extraordinary maneuvers.

2. The strongest insect: the rhinoceros beetle

- **Details:** He is capable of lifting objects 850 times his own body weight.

- **Habitat:** Tropical forests of Southeast Asia and South America.
- **Curiosity:** His strength would be equivalent to a man lifting a tank.

---

3. The largest insect: the giant wētā

- **Details:** It can reach a length of 10 cm and weigh up to 70 grams.
- **Habitat:** New Zealand.
- **Curiosity:** Despite its appearance, it is herbivorous and harmless to humans.

---

4. The insect with the shortest lifespan: the mayfly

- **Details:** It lives only for 24 hours in the adult stage.
- **Habitat:** Freshwater streams around the world.
- **Curiosity:** Its short adult life is entirely dedicated to reproduction.

---

5. The longest-living insect: the queen of the African termite

- **Details:** It can live up to 50 years, much longer than any other insect.
- **Habitat:** African savannas and forests.
- **Curiosity:** It spends its entire life inside the nest, producing millions of eggs.

---

6. The noisiest insect: the cicada

- **Details:** The singing of some species can reach 120 decibels, equal to the noise of a rock concert.
- **Habitat:** Forests and temperate areas around the world.

- **Curiosity:** Only males sing, using a membrane called a timbale.

---

7. The insect with the longest flight: the globe dragonfly

- **Details:** It migrates for over 18,000 km, crossing oceans and continents.
- **Habitat:** Spread all over the world.
- **Curiosity:** It is considered the longest migration of any insect.

---

8. The smallest insect: the fairy wasp

- **Details:** It measures just 0.139 mm, thinner than a human hair.
- **Habitat:** Tropical forests.
- **Curiosity:** It is so small that it can live inside the eggs of other insects.

---

9. The insect with the most painful bite: the bullet ant

- **Details:** Its bite causes intense pain that can last up to 24 hours.
- **Habitat:** Rainforests of Central and South America.
- **Curiosity:** Its name comes from the fact that the bite is comparable to a bullet hit.

---

10. The insect with the most powerful poison: the banana spider

- **Details:** Although it is technically an arachnid, it is often considered an insect due to its structure.
- **Habitat:** South American rainforests.
- **Curiosity:** Its venom is being studied for medical uses, such as the treatment of erectile dysfunction.

11. The most social insect: the leafcutter ant

- **Details:** Colonies can house millions of individuals, each with specific roles.
- **Habitat:** Rainforests of Central and South America.
- **Curiosity:** They grow mushrooms using the leaves as a substrate.

12. The insect with the largest wings: the Queen Alexandra butterfly

- **Details:** The wingspan can exceed 30 cm.
- **Habitat:** Rainforests of Papua New Guinea.
- **Curiosity:** It is one of the rarest and most protected butterflies in the world.

13. The most cold-resistant insect: the snow cricket

- **Details:** It can survive temperatures below -40°C.
- **Habitat:** Arctic and Alpine regions.
- **Curiosity:** It produces a natural antifreeze in the blood to prevent frostbite.

14. The longest-lived insect in hibernation: the periodical cicada

- **Details:** It remains in a larval state underground for 17 years before emerging.
- **Habitat:** Temperate forests of North America.
- **Curiosity:** When they emerge, they form huge swarms that cover entire regions.

15. The brightest insect: the firefly

- **Details:** Its light is produced through a chemical reaction called bioluminescence.
- **Habitat:** Forests and wetlands around the world.
- **Curiosity:** Light is used to attract partners during the mating season.

16. The insect with the longest jump: the flea

- **Details:** It can jump up to 200 times its own length.
- **Habitat:** Present in almost all terrestrial habitats.
- **Curiosity:** The force of the jump is due to an elastic tissue called resilin.

17. The insect with the best mimicry: the dry leaf phasmid

- **Details:** Its body looks identical to a leaf, complete with veins and irregular edges.
- **Habitat:** Rainforests of Southeast Asia.
- **Curiosity:** It remains motionless for hours, completely blending in with the environment.

18. The oldest insect: the dragonfly

- **Details:** The ancestors of modern dragonflies date back over 300 million years.
- **Habitat:** Wetlands and lakes around the world.
- **Curiosity:** Prehistoric dragonflies had a wingspan of over 70 cm.

19. The most poisonous insect: the giant scolopendra

- **Details:** Its venom can kill prey much larger than itself, such as small mammals.
- **Habitat:** Tropical and subtropical regions.

- **Curiosity:** It is an active and very aggressive predator.

---

20. The oldest fossilly known insect: the mosquito

- **Details:** Mosquito fossils have been found dating back 46 million years.
- **Habitat:** Spread all over the world.
- **Curiosity:** They are believed to have played an important role in the spread of diseases even in prehistoric times.

Insects show us how surprising and varied nature can be. Which of these records surprised you the most?

2.2 Plants

Introduction

Plants are the lifeblood of our planet, essential for the survival of all other life forms. They produce oxygen, regulate the climate and provide habitats for countless species. Among them we find true giants, champions of longevity and plants with extraordinary characteristics that defy the laws of nature.

2.2.1 Trees and Forests

Trees and forests represent some of the most powerful symbols of nature's resilience and beauty. Here are 20 incredible records regarding these extraordinary living beings.

---

1. The tallest tree: the Hyperion sequoia

- **Details:** At 115.92 meters tall, Hyperion is the tallest sequoia ever recorded.
- **Habitat:** Redwood National Park, California, USA.
- **Curiosity:** The height of the tree is monitored to protect the site from possible anthropogenic damage.

2. The oldest tree: the bristlecone pine (Methuselah)

- **Details:** This tree is over 4,800 years old.
- **Habitat:** Montagne White, California, USA.
- **Curiosity:** Its exact location is kept secret to protect it from vandalism.

3. The largest forest: the Amazon

- **Details:** It covers approximately 5.5 million square kilometers.
- **Habitat:** Sud America.
- **Curiosity:** It produces 20% of the earth's oxygen and is home to millions of species.

4. The oldest forest: the Daintree woodland

- **Details:** It dates back over 135 million years ago.
- **Habitat:** Queensland, Australia.
- **Curiosity:** It is one of the richest ecosystems in biodiversity in the world.

5. The tree with the largest trunk: General Sherman

- **Details:** This giant sequoia specimen has an estimated volume of 1,487 cubic meters.
- **Habitat:** Sequoia National Park, California, USA.

- **Curiosity:** Despite its enormity, it is not the tallest or oldest tree.

---

6. The widest tree: the Tule cypress

- **Details:** With a diameter of 14 meters, it is the tree with the widest trunk.
- **Habitat:** Oaxaca, Mexico.
- **Curiosity:** Its trunk is so large that it requires 30 people to surround it.

---

7. The largest submerged forest: the Great River Forest of the Amazon

- **Details:** This forest emerges during the dry season and submerges in the rainy one.
- **Habitat:** Amazon basin.
- **Curiosity:** Trees can survive completely submerged in water for months.

---

8. The tree with the deepest roots: the wild fig

- **Details:** Its roots reach depths of over 120 meters.
- **Habitat:** South Africa.
- **Curiosity:** The roots extend to seek underground aquifers.

---

9. The most resistant tree: the Baobab

- **Details:** It can live up to 3,000 years and survive in extreme drought conditions.
- **Habitat:** African savannas.
- **Curiosity:** It can store up to 120,000 liters of water in its trunk.

---

10. The tree with the largest root system: the Pando

- **Details:** A forest of genetically identical aspen trees covering 43 hectares.
- **Habitat:** Utah, USA.
- **Curiosity:** Considered a single living organism, Pando weighs approximately 6,000 tons.

---

11. The most toxic tree: the manzanillo

- **Details:** Its fruit is called the "apple of death" and can be lethal.
- **Habitat:** Caribbean and Central America.
- **Curiosity:** Sap and wood can also cause severe burns.

---

12. The forest with the most biodiversity: the Amazon rainforest

- **Details:** It contains about 10% of the living species on Earth.
- **Habitat:** Sud America.
- **Curiosity:** Some areas of the Amazon have not yet been explored by man.

---

13. The tallest tree in Asia: the Menara

- **Details:** A specimen of Shorea faguetiana that reaches 100.8 meters.
- **Habitat:** Rainforests of Borneo.
- **Curiosity:** The name "Menara" means "tower" in Malay.

---

14. The brightest tree: the strangler fig

- **Details:** Thanks to its bioluminescent flowers, it glows in the dark.
- **Habitat:** Tropical forests of Asia.

31

- **Curiosity:** Bioluminescence attracts nocturnal pollinating insects.

---

15. The oldest tree in Europe: the Hundred Horse Chestnut

- **Details:** It is estimated to be over 2,000 years old.
- **Habitat:** Sicily, Italy.
- **Curiosity:** The name derives from a legend according to which 100 knights took refuge under its branches during a storm.

---

16. The forest with the most extreme climate: the Siberian taiga

- **Details:** It faces temperatures ranging from -50°C to 30°C.
- **Habitat:** Russia, Canada, Alaska e Scandinavia.
- **Curiosity:** It is the largest boreal forest in the world.

---

17. The tree with the largest fruits: the jackfruit

- **Details:** Its fruits can weigh up to 35 kg.
- **Habitat:** Southeast Asian.
- **Curiosity:** Jackfruit is a key food source in many tropical cultures.

---

18. The fastest growing tree: giant bamboo

- **Details:** It can grow up to 91 cm per day.
- **Habitat:** Tropical and subtropical forests.
- **Curiosity:** Despite its appearance, bamboo is technically a grass.

---

19. The most photographed tree: the Madagascar baobab

- **Details:** Its iconic silhouette makes it a very popular subject.
- **Habitat:** Madagascar.
- **Curiosity:** It is often called the "upside down tree" because it appears to have roots instead of branches.

20. The tree with the most unique reproductive system: the fig

- **Details:** Its fruits develop only thanks to a specific pollinator wasp.
- **Habitat:** Tropical forests around the world.
- **Curiosity:** The relationship between the tree and the wasp is a perfect example of coevolution.

Trees and forests teach us the strength, beauty and wisdom of nature. Which of these records surprised you the most?

2.2.2 Flowers and Shrubs

Flowers and shrubs add color, scent and life to our world. Some are known for their extraordinary beauty, others for their size, their rarity or even their pungent odor. Here are 20 records that celebrate the wonders of the floral kingdom.

1. The largest flower: Rafflesia arnoldii flower

- **Details:** It can reach a diameter of 1.5 meters and weigh up to 11 kg.
- **Habitat:** Rainforests of Southeast Asia.
- **Curiosity:** It is also known as "corpse flower" due to its strong smell of rotting flesh.

2. The most fragrant flower: sambac jasmine

- **Details:** Its flowers are small but release an intense and sweet scent.
- **Habitat:** Tropical Asia.
- **Curiosity:** It is the national flower of the Philippines and Indonesia.

---

3. The most poisonous flower: the oleander

- **Details:** Every part of the oleander is toxic, including the leaves, flowers and nectar.
- **Habitat:** Tropical and subtropical regions.
- **Curiosity:** Despite its toxicity, it is widely used as an ornamental plant.

---

4. The rarest flower: Middlemist's Red

- **Details:** There are only two known specimens in the world, one in New Zealand and one in England.
- **Habitat:** Botanical Gardens.
- **Curiosity:** It was brought to Europe from China in the 19th century.

---

5. The brightest flower: Diphylleia grayi

- **Details:** Its petals become transparent when they get wet.
- **Habitat:** Wet mountains in Asia.
- **Curiosity:** It is known as the "skeleton flower" due to its transparency in the rain.

---

6. The largest shrub: the giant rhododendron

- **Details:** It can grow up to 30 meters tall.

- **Habitat:** Montagne dell'Himalaya.
- **Curiosity:** Its flowers are used in traditional medicine.

---

7. The oldest flower: Montsechia vidalii

- **Details:** A fossil of this flower dates back to about 125 million years ago.
- **Habitat:** Aquatic species that lived in freshwater lakes.
- **Curiosity:** It is considered one of the first flowers to appear on Earth.

---

8. The longest-lived shrub: creosote (King Clone)

- **Details:** A cloned specimen of creosote is over 11,700 years old.
- **Habitat:** Mojave Desert, USA.
- **Curiosity:** It reproduces by cloning itself, creating a ring of identical plants.

---

9. The fastest growing flower: the giant sunflower

- **Details:** It can grow up to 30 cm per day during the growing season.
- **Habitat:** Crops all over the world.
- **Curiosity:** Its seeds follow the sun in a movement called "heliotropism".

---

10. The flower with the heaviest pollen: the lily

- **Details:** Lily pollen grains are among the largest and heaviest.
- **Habitat:** Temperate and tropical zones.
- **Curiosity:** Pollen can permanently stain fabrics and surfaces.

11. The most cold-resistant flower: the Christmas rose (Helleborus niger)

- **Details:** It even blooms in the middle of winter with temperatures below freezing.
- **Habitat:** European mountains.
- **Curiosity:** It is often associated with Christmas legends and traditions.

12. The smelliest flower: Amorphophallus titanum

- **Details:** It is known as "corpse flower" due to its strong smell of rotten flesh.
- **Habitat:** Indonesian rainforests.
- **Curiosity:** It blooms only every 7-10 years, attracting crowds of visitors.

13. The smallest flower: Wolffia globosa

- **Details:** It measures just 1mm in diameter.
- **Habitat:** Freshwater bodies around the world.
- **Curiosity:** It is edible and is used in some Asian cuisines.

14. The shrub with the most poisonous fruits: the common yew

- **Details:** Its red berries contain highly toxic seeds.
- **Habitat:** Europe, Asia and Northern Africa.
- **Curiosity:** Despite its toxicity, the plant is used to produce anti-cancer drugs.

15. The most drought-resistant flower: the Jericho rose

- **Details:** This plant can survive years without water, reopening when hydrated.
- **Habitat:** Deserts of the Middle East and North Africa.
- **Curiosity:** It is also known as the "resurrection plant".

---

16. The most expensive flower: saffron

- **Details:** The stigmas of the crocus sativus flower are harvested to produce saffron, one of the most expensive spices in the world.
- **Habitat:** Temperate zones of Europe and Asia.
- **Curiosity:** It takes around 150 flowers to produce just one gram of saffron.

---

17. The shrub with the most toxic foliage: the castor bean

- **Details:** Its leaves and seeds contain ricin, a lethal substance.
- **Habitat:** Tropical and subtropical areas.
- **Curiosity:** Despite the toxicity, the seeds are used to produce castor oil.

---

18. The flower with the shortest bloom: the Selenicereus grandiflorus cactus

- **Details:** Its flowers last only one night before withering.
- **Habitat:** Deserts of Central America and the Caribbean.
- **Curiosity:** It is called "Queen of the Night" due to its short and spectacular flowering.

---

19. The shrub with the largest fruits: the baobab

- **Details:** Its fruits, known as "monkey bread", can weigh up to 3 kg.

- **Habitat:** African savannas.
- **Curiosity:** Fruits are rich in vitamin C and fiber.

---

20. The oldest flower cultivated by man: the sacred lotus

- **Details:** It has been cultivated for over 3,000 years in Asia.
- **Habitat:** Lakes and ponds in Asia.
- **Curiosity:** Lotus seeds can lie dormant for hundreds of years and then germinate.

Flowers and shrubs tell us stories of beauty, adaptability and wonder. Which of these records impressed you the most?

2.2.3 Carnivorous Plants

Carnivorous plants are an extraordinary example of evolutionary adaptation. These fascinating organisms have developed unique techniques for capturing and digesting insects, small animals and even microorganisms to survive in nutrient-poor environments. Here are 20 records linked to these surprising plants.

---

1. The largest carnivorous plant: Nepenthes rajah

- **Details:** Its sea squirts can hold up to 3 liters of liquid and capture prey such as rats and birds.
- **Habitat:** Borneo montane forests.
- **Curiosity:** The liquid in its sea squirts not only serves to digest prey, but also attracts small animals such as frogs to lay their eggs.

---

2. The smallest carnivorous plant: Utricularia gibba

- **Details:** Its traps measure less than a millimeter, but are incredibly efficient at catching aquatic microorganisms.
- **Habitat:** Ponds and swamps around the world.
- **Curiosity:** This plant is so small that it often grows in symbiosis with other plant species.

---

3. The carnivorous plant with the fastest trap: Aldrovanda vesiculosa

- **Details:** Its traps close in less than 0.02 seconds, faster than any other living organism.
- **Habitat:** Lakes and streams in Europe, Asia and Australia.
- **Curiosity:** This lightning-fast time is made possible by the osmotic pressure acting on the trap cells.

---

4. The oldest carnivorous plant: Archaeamphora longicervia

- **Details:** Fossils of this plant date back to around 120 million years ago.
- **Habitat:** Anciently present in China.
- **Curiosity:** It is the oldest known example of carnivorous plants in the history of the planet.

---

5. The most common carnivorous plant: Drosera rotundifolia

- **Details:** This little gem with leaves covered in adhesive tentacles is found on almost all continents.
- **Habitat:** Marshes and peat bogs.
- **Curiosity:** Its leaves release a sweet liquid to attract insects, which become trapped.

---

6. The carnivorous plant with the most complex trap: Sarracenia purpurea

- **Details:** It uses a combination of nectar, odor and wax to trap insects in its ascidians.
- **Habitat:** Wetlands of North America.
- **Curiosity:** In some ecosystems, the ascidians of this plant host small amphibians, creating a symbiotic relationship.

---

7. The rarest carnivorous plant: Nepenthes clipeata

- **Details:** There are fewer than 50 specimens left in the wild, due to the destruction of their habitat.
- **Habitat:** Borneo mountains.
- **Curiosity:** This plant grows on steep and often difficult to reach cliffs.

---

8. The carnivorous plant that catches the most prey: Dionaea muscipula (Venus flytrap)

- **Details:** Each trap can close on dozens of insects during its lifetime.
- **Habitat:** Sand marshes of the southeastern United States.
- **Curiosity:** The traps close only if stimulated several times, to avoid wasting energy.

---

9. The carnivorous plant that lives the longest: Heliamphora

- **Details:** Some species of Heliamphora can live over 20 years.
- **Habitat:** Tepui (highlands) of South America.
- **Curiosity:** They grow in extremely inhospitable environments, feeding almost exclusively on insects.

---

10. The most diverse carnivorous plant: Genus Nepenthes

- **Details:** With over 160 species, it is the most diverse genus of carnivorous plants.
- **Habitat:** Tropical forests of Southeast Asia.
- **Curiosity:** Each species has traps adapted to the prey available in its habitat.

---

11. The carnivorous plant that attracts bats: Nepenthes hemsleyana

- **Details:** It offers shelter to bats in exchange for nitrogen-rich excrement.
- **Habitat:** Tropical forests of Borneo.
- **Curiosity:** This symbiotic relationship helps the plant grow in extremely poor soil.

---

12. The most drought-resistant carnivorous plant: Drosophyllum lusitanicum

- **Details:** It is the only carnivorous plant that thrives in arid climates.
- **Habitat:** Mediterranean regions.
- **Curiosity:** Its leaves secrete a sweet nectar that attracts prey, despite the lack of water.

---

13. The most toxic carnivorous plant: Nepenthes bicalcarata

- **Details:** Some parts of this plant contain chemicals that are toxic to insects that try to escape.
- **Habitat:** Swamps and forests of Borneo.
- **Curiosity:** Its traps have "teeth" that prevent prey from escaping.

---

14. The carnivorous plant with the brightest color: Cephalotus follicularis

- **Details:** Its ascidians have bright colors ranging from red to bright green.
- **Habitat:** South Western Australia.
- **Curiosity:** The traps reflect UV light to attract insects more.

15. The most adaptable carnivorous plant: Genlisea

- **Details:** Its underground traps capture microorganisms in stagnant water.
- **Habitat:** Tropical swamps.
- **Curiosity:** It is also called the "corkscrew plant" due to the unique shape of its traps.

16. The carnivorous plant that digests the fastest: Brocchinia reducta

- **Details:** It can complete the digestive process in less than 48 hours.
- **Habitat:** Tepui of South America.
- **Curiosity:** Uses symbiotic bacteria to speed up digestion.

17. The carnivorous plant most resistant to frost: Pinguicula alpina

- **Details:** It survives sub-zero temperatures thanks to a dormancy cycle.
- **Habitat:** European Alps and Arctic regions.
- **Curiosity:** Catches insects to make up for missing nutrients in poor soils.

18. The carnivorous plant with the oldest trap: Drosera

- **Details:** It is one of the oldest carnivorous plants, with fossils dating back over 40 million years.

- **Habitat:** Wetlands on almost all continents.
- **Curiosity:** It was studied by Charles Darwin, who documented its behavior.

---

19. The carnivorous plant most visible to UV rays: Byblis

- **Details:** Its glands secrete a liquid that intensely reflects UV rays.
- **Habitat:** Northern Australia.
- **Curiosity:** Insects are attracted by the brilliance of the liquid, becoming trapped.

---

20. The most exotic carnivorous plant: Nepenthes lowii

- **Details:** It produces a sugary substance that attracts mammals such as tarsiers to feed.
- **Habitat:** Borneo.
- **Curiosity:** It is not limited to insects, but also feeds on nutrient-rich animal waste.

Carnivorous plants demonstrate that evolution can lead to extraordinary solutions for surviving in extreme environments. Which of these wonders caught your attention?

2.3 Natural Phenomena

Introduction

Nature is an unpredictable artist, capable of creating spectacular phenomena that leave humanity speechless. From volcanoes that shake the planet to storms that shape the landscape, natural phenomena represent the most fascinating and powerful side of our world. Some of these events are so extreme and extraordinary that they are remembered as unique records, demonstrating how both wonderful and unforgiving our planet can be.

2.3.1 Extreme Weather Events

The sky above us is never static: it can transform into a theater of electrifying spectacles or an arena of relentless destruction. Extreme weather events are manifestations of nature's primal force, often setting impressive records. Here are 20 of the most incredible phenomena related to the weather.

1. Highest temperature ever recorded: Furnace Creek, California

- **Details:** On July 10, 1913, the thermometer reached 56.7°C in Death Valley.
- **Habitat:** Mojave Desert, USA.
- **Curiosity:** Despite its name, Death Valley is home to several species adapted to extreme conditions.

2. Lowest temperature ever measured: Vostok, Antarctica

- **Details:** On July 21, 1983, the temperature hit -89.2°C at the Vostok research station.
- **Habitat:** Antarctic ice sheet.
- **Curiosity:** At these temperatures, even human breath can freeze instantly.

3. Heaviest rain in 24 hours: Foc-Foc, Réunion

- **Details:** In January 1966, 1,825 mm of rain fell in a single day.
- **Habitat:** Réunion Island, Indian Ocean.
- **Curiosity:** This phenomenon was caused by tropical cyclone Denise.

4. The most devastating hailstorm: Gopalganj, Bangladesh

- **Details:** In 1986, hailstones weighing 1 kg caused the deaths of 92 people.
- **Habitat:** Tropical plains of Bangladesh.
- **Curiosity:** Hail of that size can reach a falling speed of over 160 km/h.

5. The most powerful hurricane: Patricia, Pacific Ocean

- **Details:** In October 2015, Patricia reached winds of 345 km/h.
- **Habitat:** Eastern Pacific.
- **Curiosity:** Despite its intensity, the hurricane caused less damage than expected thanks to the low population density of the affected area.

6. Most destructive tornado: El Reno, Oklahoma

- **Details:** In May 2013, the tornado reached a diameter of 4.2 km, the largest ever recorded.
- **Habitat:** "Tornado Alley", USA.
- **Curiosity:** Its massive form and speed made it particularly difficult to track.

7. Heaviest snowfall in 24 hours: Silver Lake, Colorado

- **Details:** On April 14, 1921, 193 cm of snow fell in a single day.
- **Habitat:** Rocky Mountains, USA.
- **Curiosity:** The record snowfall blocked roads and railways for weeks.

8. Longest-lasting lightning storm: Lake Maracaibo, Venezuela

- **Details:** The phenomenon known as "Relámpago del Catatumbo" produces lightning almost every night, for over 200 days a year.
- **Habitat:** Lake Maracaibo basin.
- **Curiosity:** It is one of the largest sources of ozone on the planet.

---

9. The longest tropical cyclone: Freddy, Indian Ocean

- **Details:** In 2023, Cyclone Freddy lasted 37 days, traveling over 13,000 km.
- **Habitat:** Southern Indian Ocean.
- **Curiosity:** Freddy struck Madagascar and Mozambique several times, causing extensive damage.

---

10. The lowest atmospheric pressure: Typhoon Tip

- **Details:** In 1979, the pressure dropped to 870 hPa in the heart of the typhoon.
- **Habitat:** Western Pacific.
- **Curiosity:** Tip was also the largest typhoon ever observed, with a diameter of over 2,200 km.

---

11. Longest drought: Atacama, Chile

- **Details:** Some areas of the Atacama Desert have not received significant rainfall for over 500 years.
- **Habitat:** Deserto in Atacama, Sud America.
- **Curiosity:** Despite the aridity, the desert occasionally blooms after rare episodes of rain.

---

12. Largest snowstorm: USA, March 1993

- **Details:** This storm covered 26 states and affected 130 million people.
- **Habitat:** Nord America.
- **Curiosity:** It was nicknamed the "Storm of the Century" due to its scale.

---

13. Strongest wind ever recorded: Barrow Island, Australia

- **Details:** During Cyclone Olivia in 1996, a gust of 407 km/h was measured.
- **Habitat:** Indian Ocean.
- **Curiosity:** This record was only verified years later through in-depth analysis.

---

14. Largest hail: Vivian, South Dakota

- **Details:** A hailstone with a diameter of 20 cm and a weight of 878 grams was found in 2010.
- **Habitat:** USA.
- **Curiosity:** The grain had sharp protrusions, increasing its destructive potential.

---

15. The most intense thunderstorm: Kansas City, USA

- **Details:** In 2018, over 50,000 lightning strikes were recorded in a thunderstorm in less than an hour.
- **Habitat:** Central Plains of the United States.
- **Curiosity:** Lightning lit up the sky continuously, creating a surreal sight.

---

16. The most intense monsoon: Cherrapunji, India

- **Details:** During one monsoon season, over 26,000 mm of rain fell.

- **Habitat:** Meghalaya, India.
- **Curiosity:** Cherrapunji is known as one of the rainiest places in the world.

---

17. The cyclone with the highest number of victims: Bhola, Bangladesh

- **Details:** In 1970, the cyclone caused approximately 500,000 deaths.
- **Habitat:** Bay of Bengal.
- **Curiosity:** It was one of the most devastating natural disasters in modern history.

---

18. Longest heat wave: California, USA

- **Details:** In the summer of 2021, California experienced 67 consecutive days of temperatures above 40°C.
- **Habitat:** Mojave Desert.
- **Curiosity:** This wave helped spark numerous devastating fires.

---

19. The most spectacular meteorological phenomenon: Northern Lights

- **Details:** Generated by the interaction between the solar wind and the Earth's atmosphere, the aurora paints the sky with brilliant colors.
- **Habitat:** Polar regions.
- **Curiosity:** The ancients believed it was a divine sign or a battle between spirits.

---

20. Most snow accumulation in a season: Mount Baker, USA

- **Details:** During the winter of 1998-1999, over 29 meters of snow fell.
- **Habitat:** Washington State, USA.
- **Curiosity:** This record attracted thousands of skiers and snow lovers.

Extreme weather events remind us of the immense power of nature. Which of these surprised you the most?

2.3.2 Volcanoes and Earthquakes

Volcanoes and earthquakes are among the most impressive and devastating manifestations of the earth's force. These phenomena remind us that our planet is alive and constantly changing, shaping the landscape and influencing human life for millennia. Let's discover 20 records that highlight their power.

---

1. The most powerful eruption ever recorded: Tambora, Indonesia (1815)

- **Details:** The power of the eruption was such that it changed the global climate, causing the so-called "year without a summer".
- **Habitat:** Isola in Sumbawa, Indonesia.
- **Curiosity:** The eruption is estimated to have released 150 km^3 of volcanic material into the atmosphere.

---

2. The most active volcano in the world: Kilauea, Hawaii

- **Details:** Continuously active from 1983 to 2018, Kilauea produced lava flows that redefined the Hawaiian landscape.
- **Habitat:** Big Island of Hawaii.
- **Curiosity:** Kilauea lava created over 200 acres of new land.

49

3. The largest volcanic caldera: Yellowstone, USA

- **Details:** Measuring approximately 70 km long and 55 km wide, one of the most impressive in the world.
- **Habitat:** Wyoming, USA.
- **Curiosity:** Yellowstone is considered a supervolcano, with potential for a devastating eruption.

4. Highest volcano: Ojos del Salado, Chile

- **Details:** With an altitude of 6,893 meters, it is the highest volcano on Earth.
- **Habitat:** Come on Cylene.
- **Curiosity:** Despite its height, it still exhibits fumarolic activity.

5. The strongest earthquake ever measured: Valdivia, Chile (1960)

- **Details:** With a magnitude of 9.5, it was the most powerful earthquake ever recorded.
- **Habitat:** Coastal regions of Chile.
- **Curiosity:** The earthquake generated a tsunami that reached the coast of Japan.

6. The longest volcanic eruption: Mount Yasur, Vanuatu

- **Details:** Erupting constantly for at least 800 years, it is one of the Pacific's most famous natural attractions.
- **Habitat:** Tanna Island, Vanuatu.
- **Curiosity:** Locals consider the volcano sacred and often offer gifts to the mountain spirits.

7. The longest lava flow: Laki, Iceland (1783)

- **Details:** The lava flows extended for approximately 27 km, causing significant damage to agriculture.
- **Habitat:** Southern Iceland.
- **Curiosity:** Laki's eruption caused a famine that decimated a quarter of Iceland's population.

8. Longest earthquake: Sumatra, Indonesia (2004)

- **Details:** It lasted about 10 minutes and caused the devastating tsunami that hit the Indian Ocean.
- **Habitat:** Indian Ocean region.
- **Curiosity:** The magnitude was 9.1, causing over 230,000 victims.

9. The youngest volcano: Parícutin, Mexico

- **Details:** It appeared suddenly in 1943 in a corn field, growing rapidly to 424 meters.
- **Habitat:** State of Michoacán, Mexico.
- **Curiosity:** It is one of the few volcanoes documented from the beginning of its formation.

10. The earthquake with the largest fault displacement: Alaska (1964)

- **Details:** The 9.2 magnitude earthquake caused ground movements of up to 18 metres.
- **Habitat:** State of Alaska, USA.
- **Curiosity:** This event was followed by a tsunami that destroyed several coastal cities.

11. The most dangerous volcano today: Vesuvius, Italy

- **Details:** Its last eruption was in 1944, but millions of people live nearby.
- **Habitat:** Gulf of Naples, Italy.
- **Curiosity:** It is famous for the eruption of 79 AD, which destroyed Pompeii and Herculaneum.

---

12. Most Destructive Earthquake: Tangshan, China (1976)

- **Details:** With a magnitude of 7.6, it caused the deaths of over 240,000 people.
- **Habitat:** Hebei Province, China.
- **Curiosity:** The city was entirely rebuilt after the event.

---

13. The volcano with the most fluid lava: Mauna Loa, Hawaii

- **Details:** It produces extremely fluid lava flows that can travel long distances.
- **Habitat:** Big Island of Hawaii.
- **Curiosity:** It is the largest shield volcano in the world.

---

14. Deepest earthquake ever recorded: Bonin Islands, Japan

- **Details:** It occurred at a depth of 700 km below the Earth's surface.
- **Habitat:** Western Pacific.
- **Curiosity:** At this depth, the rocks are under extreme pressure.

---

15. The most devastating pyroclastic cloud: Mount Pelée, Martinique (1902)

- **Details:** The incandescent cloud destroyed the city of Saint-Pierre, killing 30,000 people in a few minutes.
- **Habitat:** Martinique island, Caribbean.

- **Curiosity:** Only two people survived the eruption.

---

16. The volcano with the largest crater: Ngorongoro, Tanzania

- **Details:** The crater measures approximately 19 km in diameter.
- **Habitat:** Ngorongoro protected area.
- **Curiosity:** Today it is a natural paradise, populated by numerous species of wildlife.

---

17. The most expensive earthquake: Tōhoku, Japan (2011)

- **Details:** It caused damage of over 235 billion dollars, the most expensive in history.
- **Habitat:** North Pacific Region.
- **Curiosity:** The event caused the Fukushima nuclear disaster.

---

18. Deadliest volcano: Mount Tambora, Indonesia

- **Details:** Over 71,000 people died directly or indirectly as a result of the 1815 eruption.
- **Habitat:** Isola in Sumbawa, Indonesia.
- **Curiosity:** Volcanic ash reduced global temperatures for years.

---

19. The most seismic zone in the world: Pacific Ring of Fire

- **Details:** This region is responsible for 90% of global earthquakes.
- **Habitat:** Pacific.
- **Curiosity:** It is home to numerous active volcanoes and geological faults.

---

20. The loudest volcanic eruption: Krakatoa, Indonesia (1883)

- **Details:** The roar was heard up to 4,800 km away.
- **Habitat:** Sunda Strait, Indonesia.
- **Curiosity:** The energy released was equivalent to 200 megatons of TNT.

Volcanoes and earthquakes teach us that the Earth is a constantly evolving organism, capable of radically transforming its surface and reminding us of our fragility in the face of its power.

2.3.3 Ocean Records

The oceans represent the blue heart of our planet, covering over 70% of the Earth's surface. They are places of incredible beauty, mystery and strength, with records that reflect both the breadth and depth of their impact on the planet. Here are 20 extraordinary records related to the oceans and their wonders.

---

1. The deepest point: Mariana Trench

- **Details:** The Challenger Deep, in the Mariana Trench, is located at a depth of approximately 10,984 meters.
- **Habitat:** Western Pacific Ocean.
- **Curiosity:** Only a few missions have reached this point, including an expedition by director James Cameron.

---

2. The strongest ocean current: Gulf Stream

- **Details:** This current transports approximately 30 million cubic meters of water per second.
- **Habitat:** North Atlantic.

- **Curiosity:** The Gulf Stream significantly affects the European climate, mitigating its winters.

---

3. Highest wave recorded: North Atlantic Ocean

- **Details:** In 2013, a 19 meter high wave was measured during a storm.
- **Habitat:** North Atlantic.
- **Curiosity:** These giant waves often form in force 10 sea conditions.

---

4. The largest coral reef: Great Barrier Reef

- **Details:** At over 2,300 kilometers in length, it is the largest living structure on the planet.
- **Habitat:** Pacific Ocean, Australia.
- **Curiosity:** It is visible from space and is home to thousands of marine species.

---

5. The warmest water temperature: Persian Gulf

- **Details:** Surface waters can reach 36°C in summer.
- **Habitat:** Persian Gulf, Middle East.
- **Curiosity:** These extreme temperatures take a toll on local marine life.

---

6. The saltiest sea: Dead Sea

- **Details:** Despite technically being a lake, the Dead Sea has a salinity of 33.7%.
- **Habitat:** Border between Jordan and Israel.
- **Curiosity:** The high salinity allows you to float effortlessly.

---

7. The deepest sea creature: Pseudoliparis swirei

- **Details:** This small fish lives at over 8,000 meters in the Mariana Trench.
- **Habitat:** Pacific Ocean.
- **Curiosity:** It is one of the organisms best adapted to the immense pressures of the ocean depths.

---

8. The longest ocean current: Antarctic Circumpolar Current

- **Details:** It surrounds Antarctica and extends for over 24,000 kilometers.
- **Habitat:** Southern Ocean.
- **Curiosity:** It is the only current that flows entirely around the globe.

---

9. Largest marine protected area: Cook Islands Marine Reserve

- **Details:** It covers approximately 1.9 million square kilometers.
- **Habitat:** South Pacific Ocean.
- **Curiosity:** It is dedicated to the conservation of marine biodiversity.

---

10. Most tsunamis: Japan

- **Details:** Located along the Pacific Ring of Fire, Japan experiences the highest number of tsunamis in the world.
- **Habitat:** Western Pacific Ocean.
- **Curiosity:** Advanced Japanese technology constantly monitors seismic activities to reduce risks.

---

11. Tallest seamount: Mauna Kea

- **Details:** If measured from the base on the ocean floor, it exceeds 10,000 meters in height.
- **Habitat:** Pacific Ocean, Hawaii.
- **Curiosity:** Its summit is also a privileged place for astronomical observatories.

---

12. The youngest ocean: Southern Ocean

- **Details:** Officially recognized in 2000, it is the most recently classified ocean.
- **Habitat:** Antarctic region.
- **Curiosity:** It contains 15% of the world's seawater.

---

13. The smallest sea: Sea of Azov

- **Details:** It covers an area of only 39,000 square kilometers.
- **Habitat:** Border between Ukraine and Russia.
- **Curiosity:** It is also one of the shallowest seas, with an average depth of only 7 meters.

---

14. The longest migration: Gray whale

- **Details:** Every year, gray whales travel approximately 20,000 kilometers between feeding and breeding areas.
- **Habitat:** Pacific Ocean.
- **Curiosity:** This migration makes them vulnerable to climate change and hunting.

---

15. Largest oceanic island: Greenland

- **Details:** Although surrounded by oceans, Greenland is classified as the largest island in the world, with an area of 2.16 million square kilometers.
- **Habitat:** Arctic Ocean and North Atlantic.

- **Curiosity:** It is covered by a huge ice cap.

---

16. The deepest ascent: Hydrothermal Vents

- **Details:** Hydrothermal vents are found at depths greater than 3,000 meters and release fluids at temperatures exceeding 400°C.
- **Habitat:** Ocean floors around the world.
- **Curiosity:** They support unique ecosystems that thrive without sunlight.

---

17. The coldest oceanic area: Southern Ocean

- **Details:** Temperatures can drop to -2°C, the freezing point of salt water.
- **Habitat:** Antarctic region.
- **Curiosity:** Despite the freezing weather, the ocean is full of life, including whales and penguins.

---

18. Longest ocean storm: Cyclone Catarina

- **Details:** This tropical cyclone lasted 29 days in the South Atlantic Ocean.
- **Habitat:** Brazilian coast.
- **Curiosity:** It was one of the rare tropical cyclones recorded in the South Atlantic.

---

19. The most diverse fauna: Coral Triangle

- **Details:** This region is home to approximately 75% of known coral species.
- **Habitat:** Western Pacific Ocean.
- **Curiosity:** It is called the "heart of marine biodiversity".

20. The largest reserve of oxygen: Pacific Ocean

- **Details:** It is the largest producer of oxygen on the planet, thanks to the phytoplankton that lives in its waters.
- **Habitat:** Pacific.
- **Curiosity:** Phytoplankton contributes more than 50% of the oxygen we breathe.

The oceans are an inexhaustible source of wonder and mystery. Their depths and vastness tell stories of life, strength and change that continue to impact every aspect of our planet.

3. Human Being

Introduction

Human beings are one of the most fascinating and complex creatures on the planet. Our bodies, minds and abilities have reached extraordinary limits, resulting in a multitude of records that celebrate the strength, adaptability and uniqueness of our species. From a physical point of view, the human variety is incredible: there are individuals who represent the extremes of height, weight and strength, and others who have achieved incredible feats thanks to their will. We explore records related to physiology, a starting point for understanding the wonderful complexity of the human body.

3.1 Physiology

Introduction

Human physiology is an intricate web of systems and functions that work in harmony to maintain life. However, within this perfectly balanced structure, there are unique cases that push the limits of the possible. From tallest to shortest, from heaviest to lightest, each body tells a different story. This section explores the records related to our physicality, highlighting the incredible variations within the human species.

3.1.1 Height and Weight

Humans can vary enormously in height and weight, creating extremes that often defy our understanding. Here are 20 unique records related to these characteristics.

---

1. Tallest man ever recorded: Robert Wadlow

- **Details:** It measured 2.72 meters. He was known as the "Giant of Alton".
- **Habitat:** United States.
- **Curiosity:** His extraordinary height was due to a medical condition known as pituitary hyperplasia.

---

2. Tallest woman ever recorded: Zeng Jinlian

- **Details:** It measured 2.48 meters.
- **Habitat:** China.
- **Curiosity:** She is the only woman to stand over 2.4 meters tall in recorded history.

---

3. The Shortest Man: Chandra Bahadur Dangi

- **Details:** At 54.6 cm tall, he was the shortest man ever recorded.
- **Habitat:** Nepal.
- **Curiosity:** He was respected in his community for his personality and determination.

4. The Shortest Woman: Jyoti Amge

- **Details:** Measures 62.8 cm.
- **Habitat:** India.
- **Curiosity:** Jyoti is also an actress and has participated in international television programs.

5. Heaviest man ever recorded: Jon Brower Minnoch

- **Details:** He weighed 635kg at his lifetime peak.
- **Habitat:** United States.
- **Curiosity:** Jon's obesity was due to a rare metabolic disorder.

6. Heaviest woman on record: Carol Yager

- **Details:** His maximum recorded weight was 544 kg.
- **Habitat:** United States.
- **Curiosity:** His condition drew attention to health problems related to obesity.

7. The lightest man: Lucía Zarate

- **Details:** He weighed just 2.1kg at the age of 17.
- **Habitat:** Mexico.
- **Curiosity:** She had primordial dwarfism, an extremely rare condition.

8. The lightest woman: Nisa Juarez

- **Details:** At birth, he weighed only 283 grams.
- **Habitat:** United States.

- **Curiosity:** Despite the odds, Nisa survived and became a symbol of medical hope.

---

9. Tallest living person: Sultan Kösen

- **Details:** It measures 2.51 meters.
- **Habitat:** Türkiye.
- **Curiosity:** Sultan needs a cane to walk due to his weak joints.

---

10. Shortest living person: Afshin Esmaeil Ghaderzadeh

- **Details:** Measures 65.24 cm.
- **Habitat:** Iran.
- **Curiosity:** He was recently certified as the shortest man in the world.

---

11. The tallest man ever in Africa: Gabriel Esteban Monjane

- **Details:** It measured 2.44 meters.
- **Habitat:** Mozambique.
- **Curiosity:** His exceptional height was accompanied by significant joint problems.

---

12. Youngest person to reach 6 feet: Broc Brown

- **Details:** At the age of 14, he was already 2.13 meters tall.
- **Habitat:** United States.
- **Curiosity:** He continued to grow rapidly due to a rare genetic condition.

---

13. The heaviest man to successfully lose weight: Khalid Bin Mohsen Shaari

- **Details:** He started at a weight of 610 kg and managed to lose over 400 kg.
- **Habitat:** Saudi Arabia.
- **Curiosity:** His transformation was possible thanks to intensive medical intervention.

14. Tallest living woman: Rumeysa Gelgi

- **Details:** It measures 2.15 meters.
- **Habitat:** Türkiye.
- **Curiosity:** He uses his notoriety to raise awareness of Weaver syndrome, a rare genetic condition.

15. Heaviest living person: Juan Pedro Franco

- **Details:** He reached a peak weight of 595kg before undergoing weight reduction surgery.
- **Habitat:** Mexico.
- **Curiosity:** His story has inspired many people to embark on a health journey.

16. Lightest Woman to Survive: Madeline Mann

- **Details:** At birth, he weighed only 280 grams.
- **Habitat:** United States.
- **Curiosity:** She grew up to lead a normal life, demonstrating human resilience.

17. Fastest Growing: Robert Wadlow

- **Details:** It grew 10 cm per year until its death.
- **Habitat:** United States.
- **Curiosity:** The uncontrolled growth caused him serious health problems.

18. Fastest Weight Loss: Ross Gardner

- **Details:** He lost 155 kg in a year through diet and physical activity.
- **Habitat:** United Kingdom.
- **Curiosity:** His transformation allowed him to significantly improve his quality of life.

19. Youngest to reach record weight: Lina Medina

- **Details:** Born weighing 2.7kg, she achieved normal growth despite a rare genetic condition.
- **Habitat:** Peru.
- **Curiosity:** Lina is famous for being the youngest mother in history at 5 years old.

20. The person with the greatest weight variation: Manuel Uribe

- **Details:** He went from a maximum weight of 560 kg to less than 200 kg.
- **Habitat:** Mexico.
- **Curiosity:** His story drew global attention to extreme weight management.

Differences in height and weight among humans show us the extraordinary ability of the human body to adapt, resist and overcome challenges. Each record tells a unique story, made up of incredible achievements and difficulties.

3.1.2 Physical Resistance

Human physical endurance is a fascinating field, where body and mind work together to overcome seemingly insurmountable limits. Through adaptation, training, and sometimes sheer determination, humans have proven themselves capable of extraordinary feats. Here are 20 records that testify to the resilience and strength of the human body.

---

1. Longest non-stop ride: Dean Karnazes

- **Details:** In 2005, he ran 560 km in 80 hours and 44 minutes without sleep.
- **Habitat:** United States.
- **Curiosity:** Dean attributes his incredible endurance to a rare muscle condition that prevents the buildup of lactic acid.

---

2. The longest static apnea: Budimir Šobat

- **Details:** In 2021, he held his breath for 24 minutes and 37 seconds.
- **Habitat:** Croatia.
- **Curiosity:** Before the attempt, he breathed pure oxygen to reduce the level of carbon dioxide in his blood.

---

3. The longest march without rest: David Kunst

- **Details:** He walked 23,250 km, completing a circumnavigation of the world on foot between 1970 and 1974.
- **Habitat:** It crossed four continents.
- **Curiosity:** During the journey, he was accompanied by a mule to carry his supplies.

---

4. The longest open sea swim: Benoît Lecomte

- **Details:** In 1998, he swam 5,700 km across the Atlantic Ocean in 73 days.
- **Habitat:** Atlantic Ocean.
- **Curiosity:** It fed exclusively on energy foods supplied by a support boat.

---

5. The longest fast: Angus Barbieri

- **Details:** In 1965, he lived without solid food for 382 days, losing 125 kg.
- **Habitat:** Scotland.
- **Curiosity:** During the fast, he consumed only water, coffee and vitamin supplements.

---

6. Longest time on ice: Josef Köberl

- **Details:** In 2020, he remained submerged in the ice for 2 hours, 30 minutes and 57 seconds.
- **Habitat:** Austria.
- **Curiosity:** He used breathing techniques to maintain body temperature.

---

7. Longest treadmill run: Marcio Villar

- **Details:** He traveled 827 km in 7 consecutive days.
- **Habitat:** Brazil.
- **Curiosity:** Marcio set the record as part of a charity fundraiser.

---

8. Fastest climb of Everest without oxygen: Kilian Jornet

- **Details:** He reached the summit in 26 hours in 2017.
- **Habitat:** Himalaya.

- **Curiosity:** Kilian uses no supplemental oxygen or fixed ropes, relying solely on his stamina.

---

9. Longest plank session: George Hood

- **Details:** In 2020, he held the plank position for 8 hours, 15 minutes and 15 seconds.
- **Habitat:** United States.
- **Curiosity:** George, a former Marine, broke the record at age 62.

---

10. The longest ultramarathon race: The Self-Transcendence 3100 Mile Race

- **Details:** Participants run 5,000 km in up to 52 days.
- **Habitat:** New York, USA.
- **Curiosity:** The race takes place along a circuit of just over 800 metres, repeated thousands of times.

---

11. The longest scuba dive: Ahmed Gabr

- **Details:** It reached a depth of 332.35 meters in 2014.
- **Habitat:** Red Sea, Egypt.
- **Curiosity:** The ascent lasted almost 15 hours to avoid decompression problems.

---

12. Longest time without sleep: Randy Gardner

- **Details:** In 1964, he stayed awake for 11 days and 25 minutes.
- **Habitat:** United States.
- **Curiosity:** Despite the sleep deprivation, he suffered no permanent damage.

---

13. The greatest distance traveled by bicycle without stopping: Christoph Strasser

- **Details:** In 2017, he covered 1,026 km in 24 hours.
- **Habitat:** Germany.
- **Curiosity:** Christoph is a multiple Race Across America champion.

---

14. Longest stay in fresh water: Diana Nyad

- **Details:** He swam for 53 consecutive hours from Cuba to Florida.
- **Habitat:** Caribbean Sea.
- **Curiosity:** He was the first person to accomplish this feat without a shark-protective cage.

---

15. Most pull-ups in 24 hours: Kenta Adachi

- **Details:** He completed 7,615 pull-ups in 2022.
- **Habitat:** Japan.
- **Curiosity:** Kenta has planned each individual series to maximize its efficiency.

---

16. La permanenza più lunga in una sauna: Timo Kaukonen

- **Details:** It resisted for 16 minutes at a temperature of 110 °C.
- **Habitat:** Finland.
- **Curiosity:** This competition was later abolished for safety reasons.

---

17. Longest barefoot run: Abel Mutai

- **Details:** He ran 100km without shoes in 2019.
- **Habitat:** Kenya.

- **Curiosity:** The feat was completed on arid and uneven terrain.

---

18. Highest unassisted jump: Javier Sotomayor

- **Details:** In 1993, he jumped 2.45 meters.
- **Habitat:** Cuba.
- **Curiosity:** His high jump record remained unbeaten for decades.

---

19. The longest kayak crossing: Aleksander Doba

- **Details:** He crossed the Atlantic in 167 days alone in 2011.
- **Habitat:** Atlantic Ocean.
- **Curiosity:** Aleksander was 65 years old when he completed the feat.

---

20. Most push-ups in 24 hours: Charles Service

- **Details:** He performed 46,001 push-ups in one day.
- **Habitat:** United States.
- **Curiosity:** Charles set the record at the age of 45, proving that endurance has no age.

These physical endurance records demonstrate how the human body, with training and dedication, can overcome limits that seem unimaginable. Each achievement is a celebration of the human spirit and its ability to face extraordinary challenges.

3.2 Talents

Introduction

Human beings are endowed with extraordinary abilities, which go beyond mere survival and manifest themselves in the unique talents that some individuals develop and refine. Speed, precision, agility and creativity are characteristics that allow everyone to stand out and achieve incredible results. In this section, we explore the human talents that defy all expectations, celebrating the extraordinary variety of abilities that make us unique.

3.2.1 Speed and Manual Skills

The hands and mind of man, in combination, have given rise to records that highlight speed and dexterity in feats ranging from simple coordination to the most advanced ingenuity. Let's discover 20 records that testify to extraordinary manual skill and human speed.

---

1. Fastest Rubik's Cube: Yusheng Du

- **Details:** It solved a standard Rubik's Cube in just 3.47 seconds.
- **Place:** China, 2018.
- **Curiosity:** Yusheng's strategy and mental preparation include hundreds of hours of training to optimize movements.

---

2. Fastest keyboard typing: Barbara Blackburn

- **Details:** He maintained a typing speed of 212 words per minute for 50 consecutive minutes.
- **Place:** United States.
- **Curiosity:** It used a special keyboard designed to maximize speed.

3. Fastest apple cutting with a sword: Muhamed Kahrimanovic

- **Details:** He cut 30 apples in 1 minute using a sword.
- **Place:** Germany.
- **Curiosity:** It is also known as "Cobra" for its lightning-fast accuracy.

4. Juggling the most balls in the air: Alex Barron

- **Details:** He kept 11 balls in the air for 23 consecutive throws.
- **Place:** United Kingdom.
- **Curiosity:** Alex has developed an advanced juggling technique to handle the large number of objects.

5. The fastest writing of the alphabet: Abdul Basit Siddiqi

- **Details:** He wrote the entire English alphabet in just 1.68 seconds.
- **Place:** Pakistan.
- **Curiosity:** His skill comes from years of training in fast, precise writing.

6. Most stacked dice with one hand: Silvio Sabba

- **Details:** He stacked 14 dice on one hand in 30 seconds.
- **Place:** Italy.
- **Curiosity:** This record requires a combination of stability and muscle control.

7. Most needles threaded in one minute: Nayanika Rani

- **Details:** He threaded 70 needles in just 60 seconds.

- **Place:** India.
- **Curiosity:** His manual dexterity was perfected through years of practice in tailoring.

---

8. Building a faster card deck: Bryan Berg

- **Details:** He built a stable card deck in less than 10 minutes.
- **Place:** United States.
- **Curiosity:** It uses a unique balancing technique that requires no glue or tape.

---

9. Most balloons inflated in one minute: Ryan Stock

- **Details:** He inflated 50 balloons in 60 seconds using only his breath.
- **Place:** Canada.
- **Curiosity:** His breathing ability is the result of training similar to that of freedivers.

---

10. Fastest time to tie your shoes: Pavan Solanki

- **Details:** He laced up both shoes in just 9.24 seconds.
- **Place:** India.
- **Curiosity:** Pavan's technique is based on memorizing movements, reducing execution time to a minimum.

---

11. Most cards dealt in one minute: Rick Smith Jr.

- **Details:** He threw 52 cards at a distance in less than 60 seconds.
- **Place:** United States.
- **Curiosity:** Rick is known for using cards as actual slashing weapons.

12. The Fastest Cake Decorating: Rachael Teufel

- **Details:** He decorated a three-layer cake in just 2 minutes.
- **Place:** United States.
- **Curiosity:** His technique is based on the simultaneous use of multiple decoration tools.

13. Fastest assembling a 500-piece puzzle: Wei Zhang

- **Details:** He completed the puzzle in 34 minutes and 24 seconds.
- **Place:** China.
- **Curiosity:** Wei uses a systematic strategy based on color categorization.

14. Most dice collected with chopsticks in one minute: Ashrita Furman

- **Details:** He collected 78 dice using only chopsticks.
- **Place:** United States.
- **Curiosity:** Ashrita holds numerous records for unique abilities.

15. The fastest detailed drawing: Stephen Wiltshire

- **Details:** He drew a panorama of London in less than 3 hours after observing it for a few minutes.
- **Place:** United Kingdom.
- **Curiosity:** Stephen has exceptional visual memory, associated with Savant syndrome.

16. Fastest Maze Solving: Mats Valk

- **Details:** He completed a complex maze in just 8.72 seconds.
- **Place:** Netherlands.
- **Curiosity:** Mats is an expert in cognitive and logical strategies.

---

17. Most Accurate Coin Toss: David Rush

- **Details:** He threw 100 coins into a glass from 1 meter away in 1 minute.
- **Place:** United States.
- **Curiosity:** David is known for his workouts that combine concentration and coordination.

---

18. Cutting coconuts with a machete faster: Prabhakar Reddy

- **Details:** He cut 50 coconuts in 2 minutes and 30 seconds.
- **Place:** India.
- **Curiosity:** Use a specially balanced machete to maintain accuracy and speed.

---

19. Fastest time to write an SMS: Neha Ramu

- **Details:** He wrote a standard 160-character SMS in just 18.19 seconds.
- **Place:** India.
- **Curiosity:** His speed was favored by constant training with virtual keyboards.

---

20. Building a Taller Lego Tower in One Minute: Kevin Hall

- **Details:** He built a 1.85 meter tall Lego tower in 60 seconds.
- **Place:** United States.
- **Curiosity:** Its strategy is based on a pre-planned modular design.

The combination of speed and precision is one of the most extraordinary qualities of human talent, capable of transforming simple gestures into exceptional records. Each record on this list demonstrates how vast the potential of human abilities is.

3.2.2 Memory and Intellectual Capacity

The human brain is an extraordinary machine, capable of processing, storing and recalling information with a speed and precision that often amazes. Some individuals have pushed their cognitive abilities to the limit, setting impressive records that demonstrate the immense potential of the human mind. Below, 20 examples that celebrate memory, concentration and extraordinary intellectual abilities.

1. Longest remembered sequence of digits: Chao Lu

- **Details:** He memorized and recited 67,890 digits of Pi in 24 hours.
- **Place:** China.
- **Curiosity:** To train, he used visualization and mental association techniques.

2. Fastest Sudoku Solving: Kota Morinishi

- **Details:** He completed an advanced level Sudoku in 1 minute and 23 seconds.
- **Place:** Japan.
- **Curiosity:** Its speed is attributed to a combination of photographic memory and advanced logic.

3. Largest amount of books read in a year: Charles Jones

- **Details:** He read 1,095 books, an average of 3 per day.
- **Place:** United States.
- **Curiosity:** Charles uses speed reading and quick memorization techniques.

---

4. Largest amount of binary numbers remembered: Rajveer Meena

- **Details:** He memorized and recited 70,000 binary digits.
- **Place:** India.
- **Curiosity:** He divided the digits into blocks to make memorization easier.

---

5. Most Impressive Photographic Memory: Stephen Wiltshire

- **Details:** After a brief helicopter flyover over New York, he drew a detailed map of the city.
- **Place:** United Kingdom.
- **Curiosity:** Stephen, suffering from Savant syndrome, has an almost perfect visual memory.

---

6. Fastest Solving a 4x4 Rubik's Cube: Max Park

- **Details:** He completed the cube in 17.42 seconds.
- **Place:** United States.
- **Curiosity:** Max is also known for his skill in other variations of the Rubik's Cube.

---

7. Most languages known: Ziad Fazah

- **Details:** He speaks 59 languages fluently.
- **Place:** Lebanon/Brazil.

- **Curiosity:** Ziad attributes his success to his passion for language learning.

---

8. The fastest mental calculation: Shakuntala Devi

- **Details:** He mentally multiplied two 13-digit numbers in 28 seconds.
- **Place:** India.
- **Curiosity:** She was known as "the human calculator".

---

9. The fastest solution to a chess problem: Garry Kasparov

- **Details:** He found a winning solution in just 6 seconds during a simultaneous discussion.
- **Place:** Russia.
- **Curiosity:** He is considered one of the greatest chess players in history.

---

10. The most developed short-term memory: Kim Peek

- **Details:** He was able to remember the entire contents of over 12,000 books.
- **Place:** United States.
- **Curiosity:** His story inspired the film "Rain Man".

---

11. Most words typed from memory in one minute: Michael Shestov

- **Details:** He typed 160 words in 60 seconds without errors.
- **Place:** Russia.
- **Curiosity:** Its precision has been honed through years of practice.

---

12. The speed reading record: Howard Berg

- **Details:** He achieved a reading speed of 25,000 words per minute.
- **Place:** United States.
- **Curiosity:** Howard uses dynamic reading techniques to improve comprehension.

---

13. Fastest Solving Complex Equations: Neelakantha Bhanu Prakash

- **Details:** He solved 10 complex equations in less than 60 seconds.
- **Place:** India.
- **Curiosity:** He is often called the "numbers genius".

---

14. Most historical information remembered: Gregory Redfern

- **Details:** He has recited key historical events from over 200 nations.
- **Place:** United Kingdom.
- **Curiosity:** Gregory uses a technique based on the "visual timeline".

---

15. Longest remembered poem: Akash Gupta

- **Details:** He recited a 10,000 word poem without any mistakes.
- **Place:** India.
- **Curiosity:** It took him six months to memorize it.

---

16. Record of quizzes completed: Kevin Ashman

- **Details:** He answered over 1,000 questions correctly in one day.
- **Place:** United Kingdom.
- **Curiosity:** Kevin is a celebrity in the game show world.

17. Most Morse codes deciphered: Julian Gregoire

- **Details:** He deciphered 500 messages in an hour.
- **Place:** Canada.
- **Curiosity:** Julian taught himself Morse code.

18. Most chess played simultaneously: Ehsan Ghaem Maghami

- **Details:** He played 604 simultaneous games in 25 hours.
- **Place:** Iran.
- **Curiosity:** He won 580 of those games, setting a new record.

19. Most scientific facts remembered: Roger Penrose

- **Details:** He memorized and explained over 2,000 scientific theories.
- **Place:** United Kingdom.
- **Curiosity:** Penrose is known for his ability to simplify complex concepts.

20. The longest lecture given by heart: Maria Gomez

- **Details:** He spoke for 36 consecutive hours without using notes.
- **Place:** Spain.
- **Curiosity:** Maria attributes her success to an associative memory system.

These records demonstrate how the human brain is an incredibly versatile and powerful resource. The intellectual and mnemonic abilities highlighted in this list are a tribute to the creativity and determination of the human mind.

3.3 Curiosities

Introduction

Human beings have always tried to express their individuality in unique and creative ways. Through practices ranging from body art to extreme modifications, humanity has found unusual and often surprising ways to distinguish itself. In this section we explore the curiosities linked to these expressions, celebrating the variety and complexity of human culture.

3.3.1 Body Art and Body Modifications

Body art and body modifications are ancient practices that reflect the history, traditions and personal passions of those who adopt them. Some have pushed these art forms to their limits, achieving extraordinary results and, sometimes, setting real records. Here are 20 records related to body art and body modifications.

1. The most tattoos on one person: Lucky Diamond Rich

- **Details:** He has 100% of his body covered in tattoos, including his eyes, gums and internal parts.
- **Place:** New Zealand.
- **Curiosity:** He started with white-on-black tattoos, later adding colors and overlapping designs.

2. The longest tattoo session: Alessandro Bonacorsi

- **Details:** He tattooed a client for 60 hours straight.
- **Place:** Italy.
- **Curiosity:** During the session, the client asked for a theme based on naturalistic landscapes.

---

3. The most piercings on one person: Elaine Davidson

- **Details:** She has over 4,225 piercings, including many in non-visible areas.
- **Place:** Brazil/UK.
- **Curiosity:** Despite her numerous piercings, Elaine claims to live a life free of pain or infection.

---

4. The heaviest earrings: Khalil Semmar

- **Details:** He wears earrings weighing a total of 15 kg.
- **Place:** France.
- **Curiosity:** He developed a special technique to balance the weight without compromising the ears.

---

5. The Most Forked Tongue: Erik Sprague (Lizardman)

- **Details:** He subjected his tongue to extreme modification to achieve a forked effect similar to that of reptiles.
- **Place:** United States.
- **Curiosity:** He is known for his reptile-inspired appearance, which includes green tattoos and filed teeth.

---

6. The largest number of implanted horns: Maria José Cristerna

- **Details:** He has over 10 subcutaneous implants that simulate horns on his head.
- **Place:** Mexico.

- **Curiosity:** Maria, nicknamed "The Vampire Woman", chose these modifications as a symbol of strength.

---

7. Largest tattoo in a single session: Hollis Cantrell

- **Details:** He completed a full back tattoo in 53 hours of continuous work.
- **Place:** United States.
- **Curiosity:** The tattoo represents a mythological scene with extremely complex details.

---

8. Most modified eyes: Luna Cobra

- **Details:** He is known for tattooing the sclera (the white part of the eye) in different colors.
- **Place:** United States.
- **Curiosity:** The technique was invented for an art project and later adopted by others.

---

9. The greatest extension of earlobes: Kalawelo Kaiwi

- **Details:** Its lobes measure 12 cm in diameter.
- **Place:** Hawaii.
- **Curiosity:** Kaiwi considers the elongated lobes a form of spiritual connection to his culture.

---

10. The largest number of subcutaneous implants: Henry Damon

- **Details:** He has over 30 subcutaneous implants on his head, arms and chest.
- **Place:** Venezuela.
- **Curiosity:** He transformed his appearance to resemble the superhero Red Skull.

11. The longest henna line: Meena Kumari

- **Details:** He created an uninterrupted 250 meter long henna design.
- **Place:** India.
- **Curiosity:** The work was completed in 12 hours and depicts scenes from Indian mythology.

12. Highest Piercing: Dirk Ashcroft

- **Details:** He has a permanent piercing on his eyebrow arch 2.5 cm from his scalp.
- **Place:** United Kingdom.
- **Curiosity:** Dirk is also an artist specializing in extreme performances.

13. Longest tattooed beard: George Troxler

- **Details:** He has a tattoo that simulates a 50 cm long beard.
- **Place:** Germany.
- **Curiosity:** George chose this art form to avoid having to maintain a real beard.

14. Largest tribal design on a body: Taupō Tamatoa

- **Details:** The tattoo covers 95% of the body and is inspired by Maori culture.
- **Place:** New Zealand.
- **Curiosity:** The work required over 300 hours of work.

15. The Longest Decorated Nails: Lee Redmond

- **Details:** It has decorated nails up to 90 cm long.
- **Place:** United States.
- **Curiosity:** Each nail is painted with artistic details that change seasonally.

---

16. The widest decorative scar: Nuala Cred

- **Details:** The artistic scar covers his entire back and is inspired by a Chinese dragon.
- **Place:** United Kingdom.
- **Curiosity:** Healing was achieved with advanced techniques to maintain a crisp design.

---

17. The largest number of teeth decorated with gems: Juan Moreno

- **Details:** It has 20 teeth decorated with precious stones.
- **Place:** Spain.
- **Curiosity:** The gems are set with specialized dental techniques.

---

18. Most temporary tattoos applied in one hour: Lisa Garcia

- **Details:** He applied 670 temporary tattoos in 60 minutes.
- **Place:** United States.
- **Curiosity:** The tattoos were done on volunteers during a charity event.

---

19. The widest color scale of body painting: Sophie Green

- **Details:** He painted a human body using 250 different shades.
- **Place:** Australia.

- **Curiosity:** The project was carried out as part of an art awareness campaign.

---

20. **The greatest number of rings on an elongated neck: Mya Naung**

- **Details:** He wears 20 rings on his neck, lengthening it by more than 15 cm.
- **Place:** Myanmar.
- **Curiosity:** The practice is part of a cultural tradition of Padaung women.

Body art and body modifications are not only a means of beautifying the body, but also a form of personal and cultural expression that tells unique and often surprising stories. Each record represents a journey of transformation and creativity.

3.3.2 Unique and Unexpected Records

There are records that escape any traditional category, surprising for their originality and, sometimes, for their eccentric character. These extraordinary records, often the fruit of passion and imagination, show that there is no limit to the possibilities of human ingenuity. Below, a selection of 20 truly unique and unexpected records.

---

1. **The most balanced spoons on the face: Dalibor Jablanovic**

- **Details:** He balanced 31 spoons on his face at once.
- **Place:** Serbia.
- **Curiosity:** Dalibor discovered his talent as a child and perfected it over time.

2. The most straws in your mouth: Simon Elmore

- **Details:** He held 400 straws in his mouth for 10 seconds without the help of his hands.
- **Place:** Germany.
- **Curiosity:** He spent months training to compress the straws without breaking them.

3. Longest Leap in a Burlap Bag: Ashrita Furman

- **Details:** He covered 5km by jumping into a jute bag in less than an hour.
- **Place:** United States.
- **Curiosity:** Ashrita holds numerous eccentric records due to her creativity.

4. Longest frisbee game on a mountain: Daniel Kositzke

- **Details:** He threw a Frisbee for 24 straight hours on the summit of Mount Rainer.
- **Place:** United States.
- **Curiosity:** The thin air made it more difficult to maintain the precision of the launches.

5. Most keys turned in one minute: Peter Dowdeswell

- **Details:** He turned 120 keys in 60 seconds.
- **Place:** United Kingdom.
- **Curiosity:** Peter is an expert in manual speed challenges.

6. The tallest popcorn building: Fabiano Villani

- **Details:** He made a 3.5 meter tall popcorn tower.
- **Place:** Brazil.
- **Curiosity:** The structure was built without using glue or supports, just stuck popcorn.

---

7. The longest line of fallen dominators: Sinners Domino Entertainment

- **Details:** They knocked over 4,491,863 dominoes in a spectacular sequence.
- **Place:** Germany.
- **Curiosity:** The preparation of the line required over two months of work.

---

8. Most paintbrushes held in one hand: Eric Finley

- **Details:** He held 115 brushes in one hand without dropping them.
- **Place:** United States.
- **Curiosity:** He developed this skill as an artist, working with excess materials.

---

9. Most Nose Balloons: Andrew Dahl

- **Details:** He inflated 23 balloons in 3 minutes using only his nostrils.
- **Place:** United States.
- **Curiosity:** Andrew refined his breathing technique to reduce fatigue.

---

10. Longest time spent spinning a hula hoop: Aaron Hibbs

- **Details:** He spun a hula hoop for 74 hours straight.
- **Place:** United States.

- **Curiosity:** Throughout the test, Aaron maintained a steady pace to avoid dizziness.

---

11. Largest collection of rubber ducks: Charlotte Lee

- **Details:** He has over 9,000 different ducks.
- **Place:** United States.
- **Curiosity:** His collection started as a hobby and turned into a true passion.

---

12. Most shirts worn at one time: Sanath Bandara

- **Details:** He wore 257 t-shirts one on top of the other.
- **Place:** Sri Lanka.
- **Curiosity:** It took Sanath over 6 hours to complete the dressing.

---

13. Longest row of chin-balanced chairs: Ashrita Furman

- **Details:** He balanced 15 chairs for 10 seconds.
- **Place:** United States.
- **Curiosity:** To achieve this record, he used carefully calibrated wooden chairs.

---

14. The most number of hanging apple bites: Li Xiaomeng

- **Details:** He took 65 bites of suspended apples in 60 seconds.
- **Place:** China.
- **Curiosity:** He has developed a rapid technique for biting without stopping.

---

15. The most balls thrown and caught with the feet: Yang Zhiyun

- **Details:** He threw and caught 32 balls in one minute using only his feet.
- **Place:** China.
- **Curiosity:** This skill arose as part of a circus performance.

---

16. Most meshes stuck in a fishing net in one hour: Maria Kovalenko

- **Details:** He completed 300 stitches in 60 minutes.
- **Place:** Ukraine.
- **Curiosity:** Maria learned this art since she was a child, perfecting her speed.

---

17. Tallest Bottle Cap Construction: Mark Thompson

- **Details:** He created a 12 meter tall tower using only bottle caps.
- **Place:** United Kingdom.
- **Curiosity:** The structure was assembled without adhesives, exploiting only the balance.

---

18. The longest backward march: Xu Zhenhua

- **Details:** He walked 500 km backwards in 10 days.
- **Place:** China.
- **Curiosity:** Xu used mirrors to maintain control while driving.

---

19. Most eggs carried with a spoon: Lily Zhang

- **Details:** He carried 120 eggs with a spoon in 5 minutes without breaking any.
- **Place:** Singapore.
- **Curiosity:** His technique includes a perfect balance between speed and control.

20. The longest time spent under a rain of milk: Giovanni Luca

- **Details:** He remained under a continuous flow of milk for 3 hours.
- **Place:** Italy.
- **Curiosity:** This record was set to raise awareness of the value of food.

These records demonstrate that, with creativity and passion, extraordinary feats can be achieved even in the most unexpected contexts. Each record tells a story of originality and dedication.

4. Science and Technology

Introduction

Science and technology are the engine of human progress. Thanks to research and innovation, humanity has achieved extraordinary goals, overcoming barriers considered insurmountable and profoundly transforming our way of life. From the edges of the universe to the depths of the artificial mind, this section explores the most extraordinary records linked to the scientific and technological world.

4.1 Technology

Introduction

Technology is a reflection of the human ability to solve problems and shape the future. Every innovation comes from the desire to improve life, and technological records represent the culmination of this collective effort. From artificial intelligence to robotics, these feats not only demonstrate human ingenuity, but also define new possibilities for our future.

4.1.1 Robots and Artificial Intelligence

Robotics and artificial intelligence (AI) are fields that have revolutionized numerous sectors, from medicine to logistics, from creativity to space research. These records show how machines are redefining what is possible, pushing the limits of technology to new levels.

1. The fastest robot: Cheetah

- **Details:** It reaches a speed of 28.3 miles per hour (approximately 45.5 km/h).
- **Place:** Boston Dynamics Laboratory, USA.
- **Curiosity:** It was designed to simulate the fluid movement of a cheetah, with applications for rescue and military operations.

2. The most advanced AI in the game of chess: AlphaZero

- **Details:** Defeated previous AI champion Stockfish after just 4 hours of self-learning.
- **Place:** DeepMind, UK.
- **Curiosity:** AlphaZero uses an intuition-based approach, similar to the human one, but with unparalleled speed.

3. The most realistic humanoid robot: Ameca

- **Details:** It features extremely natural facial expressions and advanced conversational interactions.
- **Place:** United Kingdom.

- **Curiosity:** Ameca is designed to study and improve human-machine interaction.

---

4. The smallest drone: RoboBee

- **Details:** It measures just 3 cm and weighs less than 1 gram.
- **Place:** Harvard University, USA.
- **Curiosity:** It is designed to pollinate plants and monitor hard-to-reach environments.

---

5. Most synchronized robots: Ever Win Company

- **Details:** It synchronized 1,069 robots in a coordinated choreography.
- **Place:** China.
- **Curiosity:** Each robot was programmed to dance without interfering with the others.

---

6. The most precise robotic arm: Da Vinci Surgical System

- **Details:** It can operate with micrometric precision, allowing minimally invasive surgeries.
- **Place:** United States.
- **Curiosity:** It is used in thousands of hospitals around the world to improve surgical outcomes.

---

7. The most creative AI: DALL-E

- **Details:** It is able to generate highly realistic images starting from textual descriptions.
- **Place:** OpenAI, USA.
- **Curiosity:** The name DALL-E is a play on words that combines Salvador Dalí and WALL-E, the famous Disney robot.

8. The toughest underwater robot: Boaty McBoatface

- **Details:** It can operate up to a depth of 6,000 meters.
- **Place:** United Kingdom.
- **Curiosity:** It has been used to study ocean currents and their impact on climate.

9. The fastest industrial robot: FANUC M-1iA

- **Details:** It is capable of carrying out 120 operations per minute.
- **Place:** Japan.
- **Curiosity:** This robot is mainly used in the assembly of electronic components.

10. Longest conversation with a chatbot: Xiaoice

- **Details:** One user talked to Xiaoice for over 29 consecutive hours.
- **Place:** China.
- **Curiosity:** Xiaoice is famous for his empathetic conversation style and "human" tone.

11. The robot with the highest learning ability: Sophia

- **Details:** He is a humanoid robot capable of learning from his dialogues and adapting to new conversations.
- **Place:** Hanson Robotics, Hong Kong.
- **Curiosity:** Sophia was the first car to receive citizenship of a state (Saudi Arabia).

12. The most accurate AI in medical diagnosis: IBM Watson

- **Details:** It has an accuracy of over 90% in identifying complex diseases.
- **Place:** USA.
- **Curiosity:** Watson is used in hospitals to support doctors in analyzing large amounts of clinical data.

---

13. The smallest robot used in surgery: Origami Robot

- **Details:** It can be ingested to perform minimally invasive internal procedures.
- **Place:** WHAT, USA.
- **Curiosity:** It folds like origami to move inside the human body.

---

14. The first robot orchestra: Toyota Partner Robots

- **Details:** They played classical music using real instruments such as violins and trumpets.
- **Place:** Japan.
- **Curiosity:** The orchestra was created to showcase the evolution of robotics in the entertainment field.

---

15. The robot that traveled the longest distance: Opportunity

- **Details:** It traveled 45.16 km on the surface of Mars during its 15 years of operation.
- **Place:** Planet Mars.
- **Curiosity:** It was only designed to last 90 days, but it far exceeded expectations.

---

16. The most efficient AI in facial recognition: Face++

- **Details:** It has 99.8% accuracy in human face recognition.
- **Place:** China.

- **Curiosity:** It is used in security and personal identification applications.

---

17. The most versatile food processor: Thermomix TM6

- **Details:** It can perform over 20 functions, from cooking to weighing.
- **Place:** Germany.
- **Curiosity:** It is one of the most innovative appliances on the market, loved by professional and amateur chefs.

---

18. The longest-lived robot in space: Voyager 1

- **Details:** It has been operational for over 45 years, transmitting data from interstellar space.
- **Place:** Interstellar space.
- **Curiosity:** Voyager 1 is the most distant human object from Earth.

---

19. The heaviest robot: BigDog

- **Details:** It weighs 109kg and is designed to carry heavy loads in difficult terrain.
- **Place:** United States.
- **Curiosity:** It was developed to assist the military in extreme situations.

---

20. The robot with the best emotional learning ability: Pepper

- **Details:** It is able to recognize human emotions and respond accordingly.
- **Place:** SoftBank Robotics, Giappone.
- **Curiosity:** Pepper is used in educational, commercial and healthcare contexts to improve interaction with people.

Robotics and artificial intelligence represent the future of technology, demonstrating how far we can go in creating machines that help us understand and transform the world we live in.

4.1.2 Space Innovations

Space exploration is one of the most extraordinary undertakings ever undertaken by humanity. Technological innovations developed to explore the cosmos have not only expanded our understanding of the universe, but have also led to significant advances in many other areas. Below, 20 records that celebrate the most surprising achievements in space innovation.

1. The longest space mission: Valeri Polyakov

- **Details:** He spent 437 consecutive days aboard the Mir space station.
- **Place:** Earth orbit.
- **Curiosity:** During the mission, Polyakov completed over 7,000 orbits around the Earth.

2. The most powerful space launch: Saturn V

- **Details:** This rocket generated thrust of 35 million Newtons.
- **Place:** United States.
- **Curiosity:** It was used for the Apollo missions, including the one that put the first man on the Moon.

3. Fastest spacecraft: Parker Solar Probe

- **Details:** It reached a speed of over 700,000 km/h as it approached the Sun.
- **Place:** Interplanetary space.
- **Curiosity:** The probe is designed to withstand temperatures above 1,300°C.

---

4. The first human object in space: Sputnik 1

- **Details:** This satellite was launched by the Soviet Union on October 4, 1957.
- **Place:** Earth orbit.
- **Curiosity:** The success of Sputnik started the space race.

---

5. The mission with the most astronauts: STS-61-A

- **Details:** The Space Shuttle Challenger carried 8 astronauts in 1985.
- **Place:** Earth orbit.
- **Curiosity:** This mission was an example of international cooperation, with astronauts of different nationalities.

---

6. The largest space station: ISS (International Space Station)

- **Details:** It measures over 100 meters in length and weighs approximately 420 tons.
- **Place:** Earth orbit.
- **Curiosity:** The ISS was assembled in space by several nations and has been continuously inhabited since 2000.

---

7. The most powerful space telescope: James Webb Space Telescope

- **Details:** With its 6.5-meter primary mirror, it can observe galaxies that formed over 13 billion years ago.

- **Place:** Lagrange point L2, deep space.
- **Curiosity:** It is the successor to the famous Hubble and uses advanced technologies to observe infrared.

---

8. The first human footprint on the Moon: Neil Armstrong

- **Details:** The American astronaut was the first to walk on the lunar surface on July 20, 1969.
- **Place:** Sea of Tranquility, Moon.
- **Curiosity:** The phrase "One small step for a man, one giant leap for mankind" has become iconic.

---

9. The rover with the longest operational life: Opportunity

- **Details:** Designed to last 90 days, it has worked for over 15 years.
- **Place:** Planet Mars.
- **Curiosity:** It traveled over 45 km on the Martian surface, setting a record for an extraterrestrial vehicle.

---

10. The first photo of Earth from space: V-2 Rocket

- **Details:** Taken in 1946 by a V-2 rocket, this image changed humanity's perception of their planet.
- **Place:** Suborbit of Earth.
- **Curiosity:** The photo showed a large portion of New Mexico territory.

---

11. The first asteroid landing: Hayabusa

- **Details:** This Japanese probe landed on the asteroid Itokawa in 2005.
- **Place:** Interplanetary space.

- **Curiosity:** It brought samples of the asteroid back to Earth, contributing to the study of the formation of the solar system.

---

12. Longest human stay in deep space: Apollo 17

- **Details:** The Apollo 17 astronauts spent 12 days in space, including 3 days on the Moon.
- **Place:** Deep space.
- **Curiosity:** It was the last human mission to the Moon.

---

13. The farthest artificial satellite: Voyager 1

- **Details:** It is currently over 23 billion kilometers from Earth.
- **Place:** Interstellar space.
- **Curiosity:** Contains a golden disc with sounds and images of Earth, intended for potential extraterrestrial civilizations.

---

14. The cheapest launch: PSLV-C37

- **Details:** It put 104 satellites into orbit at a cost of just $15 million.
- **Place:** India.
- **Curiosity:** It set a record for the most satellites launched in a single flight.

---

15. The longest interplanetary mission: New Horizons

- **Details:** It took 9 years to reach Pluto and send back detailed images of the dwarf planet.
- **Place:** Outer solar system.
- **Curiosity:** The mission continues to explore the Kuiper Belt.

---

16. The lowest temperature ever reached in space: Cold Atom Laboratory

- **Details:** It created conditions near absolute zero (-273.15°C) to study quantum physics.
- **Place:** ISS.
- **Curiosity:** This innovation allows us to explore phenomena that are impossible to observe on Earth.

---

17. Fastest launch to Mars: Tianwen-1

- **Details:** The Chinese mission reached the red planet in just 202 days.
- **Place:** Dinner/Tuesday.
- **Curiosity:** Tianwen-1 includes a rover, an orbiter and a lander, all operating simultaneously.

---

18. Largest impact crater studied: Chicxulub

- **Details:** This crater, 150 km wide, was studied through drilling carried out from the sea.
- **Place:** Yucatán Peninsula, Mexico.
- **Curiosity:** The impact that generated it is believed to have caused the extinction of the dinosaurs.

---

19. The most advanced reusable rocket: Falcon 9

- **Details:** It can be launched and recovered multiple times, significantly reducing mission costs.
- **Place:** United States.
- **Curiosity:** SpaceX has used Falcon 9 for commercial, government and humanitarian missions.

---

20. The most ambitious project: Gateway

- **Details:** This space station, still under construction, will orbit the Moon as a base for future space missions.
- **Place:** Lunar orbit.
- **Curiosity:** Gateway will serve as a launchpad for the exploration of Mars and beyond.

Space exploration continues to push the limits of science and technology, offering an unprecedented glimpse into the universe and inspiring new generations to look beyond the confines of Earth.

4.1.3 Renewable Energy and Sustainable Technologies

Innovations in renewable energy and sustainable technologies are shaping the future of our planet. These solutions, designed to reduce environmental impact and improve energy efficiency, are achieving extraordinary goals. Below, 20 records that demonstrate how science and technology can contribute to a more sustainable world.

---

1. Largest solar power plant: Bhadla Solar Park

- **Details:** Located in India, it covers an area of 56 km² with a capacity of 2,245 MW.
- **Place:** Rajasthan, India.
- **Curiosity:** This solar park provides clean energy to millions of families.

---

2. The highest efficiency of a solar panel: Heterojunction Solar Cell

- **Details:** It achieved a record efficiency of 47.1% under laboratory conditions.
- **Place:** Swiss.

- **Curiosity:** This technology combines traditional solar cells and innovative materials.

---

3. The largest wind turbine: Siemens Gamesa SG 14-222 DD

- **Details:** With blades 108 meters long, it can generate 15 MW of energy.
- **Place:** Denmark.
- **Curiosity:** A single turbine can power 18,000 European homes.

---

4. The first country to use only renewable energy for a year: Costa Rica

- **Details:** In 2015, the country produced 100% of its energy from renewable sources for 300 consecutive days.
- **Place:** Costa Rica.
- **Curiosity:** This result was achieved thanks to hydroelectric, wind, solar and geothermal energy.

---

5. The largest battery in the world: Moss Landing Energy Storage

- **Details:** This lithium-ion battery has a capacity of 1,200 MW/h.
- **Place:** California, USA.
- **Curiosity:** It can provide backup power to over 300,000 homes for 4 hours.

---

6. The tallest wind turbine: Max Bögl Wind AG

- **Details:** With a height of 246.5 meters, it is located on a concrete tower with a hydroelectric reservoir at the base.
- **Place:** Germany.

- **Curiosity:** Combine wind and hydropower to maximize production.

---

7. Largest offshore wind farm: Hornsea 2

- **Details:** It has a capacity of 1,386 MW and is located in the North Sea.
- **Place:** United Kingdom.
- **Curiosity:** Its turbines are as tall as the Empire State Building.

---

8. The first airplane flight powered by solar energy: Solar Impulse 2

- **Details:** It circumnavigated the globe in 2016 without using fossil fuels.
- **Place:** Global.
- **Curiosity:** The plane was covered in 17,248 solar cells.

---

9. The largest geothermal power plant: The Geysers

- **Details:** It has a capacity of 1,590 MW and is located in California.
- **Place:** USA.
- **Curiosity:** It provides clean energy to the entire surrounding region.

---

10. The most sustainable city: Masdar City

- **Details:** Designed to be a zero-emission city, it uses solar energy and electric transport systems.
- **Place:** Abu Dhabi, Emirati Arab Uniti.
- **Curiosity:** It is considered a laboratory for sustainable urbanization.

11. Highest number of trees planted in one day: Green India Challenge

- **Details:** Over 66 million trees were planted in 12 hours.
- **Place:** India.
- **Curiosity:** This record aims to fight climate change and deforestation.

12. Largest carbon capture facility: Orca

- **Details:** It can capture 4,000 tons of CO_2 per year.
- **Place:** Iceland.
- **Curiosity:** The captured CO_2 is transformed into rock through natural chemical processes.

13. The longest high voltage electricity grid: Rio Madeira HVDC

- **Details:** With a length of 2,375 km, it transports energy from hydroelectric plants in the Amazon to southern Brazil.
- **Place:** Brazil.
- **Curiosity:** This network uses HVDC technology to reduce energy loss.

14. Largest solar-powered desalination plant: Ras Al Khair

- **Details:** It produces 1,025 million liters of drinking water per day.
- **Place:** Saudi Arabia.
- **Curiosity:** Combine solar and electric energy to make desalination more sustainable.

15. Highest e-waste recycling capacity: Umicore

- **Details:** Recycles 350,000 tons of e-waste per year.
- **Place:** Belgium.
- **Curiosity:** Recover precious metals such as gold, silver and platinum.

---

16. The first hydrogen-powered train: Coradia iLint

- **Details:** It runs on hydrogen fuel cells, emitting only water vapor.
- **Place:** Germany.
- **Curiosity:** It is an innovation for sustainable rail transport.

---

17. The largest vertical forest: Vertical Forest

- **Details:** Two towers in Milan host over 900 trees and 20,000 plants.
- **Place:** Italy.
- **Curiosity:** This project reduces urban pollution and improves air quality.

---

18. Most solar panels on a building: Apple Park

- **Details:** Apple's headquarters in Cupertino is covered by 17 MW of solar panels.
- **Place:** United States.
- **Curiosity:** It is one of the most sustainable buildings in the world.

---

19. Highest percentage of renewable energy: Iceland

- **Details:** The country produces 100% of its electricity from renewable sources.
- **Place:** Iceland.

- **Curiosity:** Geothermal and hydroelectric energy are the main sources.

---

20. The largest biogas plant: EnviTec Biogas

- **Details:** It has a capacity of 140 MW, transforming organic waste into energy.
- **Place:** Germany.
- **Curiosity:** This plant provides enough energy to power a medium-sized city.

Innovations in the field of renewable energy and sustainable technologies represent a concrete commitment towards a greener and more sustainable future. Every record is a step forward in the fight against climate change and for improving the global quality of life.

4.2 Science

Introduction

Science is the pillar of human knowledge, the means through which we explore, understand and transform the world around us. From the infinitely small to the majestic universe, each discovery pushes us towards new horizons. In this section, we celebrate the scientific records that have defined our understanding of reality, giving rise to extraordinary achievements and revolutionary innovations.

4.2.1 Astronomy

Astronomy is one of the oldest sciences, born from the observation of the stars and their arrangement in the sky. Over millennia, humans have developed increasingly advanced tools and methods to explore the cosmos. Below, 20 extraordinary records related to astronomy and the discovery of deep space.

---

1. The most distant galaxy ever observed: GN-z11

- **Details:** Located 13.4 billion light-years from Earth, this galaxy formed about 400 million years after the Big Bang.
- **Place:** Deep space.
- **Curiosity:** The discovery was possible thanks to the Hubble Space Telescope.

---

2. The brightest star: R136a1

- **Details:** It has a brightness equivalent to 8.7 million suns.
- **Place:** Large Magellanic Cloud.
- **Curiosity:** It is also one of the most massive stars ever discovered, with a mass 315 times that of the Sun.

---

3. The nearest exoplanet: Proxima Centauri b

- **Details:** It orbits Proxima Centauri, the closest star to our solar system.
- **Place:** 4.2 light years from Earth.
- **Curiosity:** It is a candidate for the search for extraterrestrial life due to its location in the habitable zone.

---

4. The largest black hole: TON 618

- **Details:** It has a mass approximately 66 billion times that of the Sun.
- **Place:** Deep space.
- **Curiosity:** This black hole is an ultra-luminous quasar that shines thanks to material falling into it.

5. Most exoplanets discovered: Kepler Space Telescope

- **Details:** It has identified over 2,600 planets outside our solar system.
- **Place:** Deep space.
- **Curiosity:** The Kepler mission revolutionized our understanding of the habitable universe.

6. The closest star to the Sun: Proxima Centauri

- **Details:** It is located at a distance of 4.24 light years.
- **Place:** Alpha Centauri system.
- **Curiosity:** It is a red dwarf with highly variable solar activity.

7. The largest optical telescope: Gran Telescopio Canarias

- **Details:** It has a main mirror of 10.4 meters in diameter.
- **Place:** Canary Islands, Spain.
- **Curiosity:** It is used to observe stars, galaxies and cosmic phenomena at great distances.

8. The hottest planet: KELT-9b

- **Details:** Its surface temperature reaches 4,300 °C, hotter than many stars.
- **Place:** 650 light years from Earth.
- **Curiosity:** KELT-9b is a gas giant that orbits very close to its star.

9. The fastest natural object: Neutron star PSR J1748-2446ad

- **Details:** It rotates on itself at a speed of 716 revolutions per second.
- **Place:** Sagittarius constellation.
- **Curiosity:** It is one of the densest and most compact neutron stars ever observed.

---

10. The largest number of moons of a planet: Saturn

- **Details:** It has 83 confirmed moons, surpassing Jupiter in the tally.
- **Place:** Solar system.
- **Curiosity:** Titan, one of its moons, is the only one with a dense atmosphere and liquid seas.

---

11. The largest cosmic structure: Great Wall of Hercules-Corona Borealis

- **Details:** It extends over 10 billion light years.
- **Place:** Deep space.
- **Curiosity:** This structure challenges current theories about the uniform distribution of matter in the universe.

---

12. The largest impact crater in the solar system: Hellas Crater

- **Details:** It has a diameter of 2,300 km and a depth of 7 km.
- **Place:** Planet Mars.
- **Curiosity:** The crater is also visible with ground-based telescopes.

---

13. The largest number of stars in a galaxy: IC 1101

- **Details:** It contains approximately 100 trillion stars.
- **Place:** Constellation of Virgo.
- **Curiosity:** It is one of the largest galaxies ever discovered.

14. The largest asteroid: Ceres

- **Details:** It has a diameter of 940 km and is also classified as a dwarf planet.
- **Place:** Asteroid belt.
- **Curiosity:** Ceres has ice deposits that may contain traces of microbial life.

15. The oldest star: SMSS J031300.36-670839.3

- **Details:** It formed about 13.8 billion years ago, shortly after the Big Bang.
- **Place:** Milky Way.
- **Curiosity:** Its chemical composition is poor in metals, typical of early stars.

16. The first black hole photographed: M87*

- **Details:** It was captured by the Event Horizon Telescope in 2019.
- **Place:** Messier 87 Galaxy.
- **Curiosity:** The image shows the black hole's shadow surrounded by a bright ring of material.

17. The largest planet: HD 100546 b

- **Details:** It has a mass 20 times greater than that of Jupiter.
- **Place:** 320 light years from Earth.
- **Curiosity:** It is a planet in formation, surrounded by a disk of gas and dust.

18. The highest temperature ever measured in the Sun: Solar Corona

- **Details:** It reaches temperatures of 15 million °C.
- **Place:** Solar system.
- **Curiosity:** This temperature is higher than the surface of the Sun, a feature still being studied.

---

19. The brightest supernova: SN 2006gy

- **Details:** It was 50 times brighter than a typical supernova.
- **Place:** 240 million light years from Earth.
- **Curiosity:** It was caused by the explosion of a massive star rich in heavy elements.

---

20. The most recent discovery: TRAPPIST-1

- **Details:** A planetary system with 7 Earth-like planets, 3 of which are in the habitable zone.
- **Place:** 39 light years from Earth.
- **Curiosity:** It is one of the best candidates for the search for extraterrestrial life.

Astronomy allows us to look beyond our world and better understand our place in the universe. Each record is a step forward in the great adventure of cosmic knowledge.

4.2.2 Medicine

Medicine is an ever-evolving field, where science and innovation come together to improve human health and quality of life. From pioneering interventions to groundbreaking discoveries, each record represents a milestone in the history of medical science. Here are 20 extraordinary records that have redefined the boundaries of medicine.

---

1. The first human heart transplant: Christiaan Barnard

- **Details:** In 1967, the South African surgeon performed the first heart transplant on a 53-year-old patient.
- **Place:** South Africa.
- **Curiosity:** Although the patient survived only 18 days, the surgery paved the way for modern transplant surgery.

---

2. Longest survival after a heart transplant: John McCafferty

- **Details:** He lived 33 years after receiving a heart transplant.
- **Place:** United Kingdom.
- **Curiosity:** John attributed his longevity to a healthy lifestyle and advances in post-transplant medicine.

---

3. The first vaccine developed: Edward Jenner

- **Details:** In 1796, Jenner created the first smallpox vaccine.
- **Place:** United Kingdom.
- **Curiosity:** Its discovery led to the eradication of smallpox in 1980.

---

4. The most complex organ transplant: complete face

- **Details:** In 2018, a medical team performed a full face transplant on a severely disfigured patient.
- **Place:** United States.
- **Curiosity:** The operation lasted 25 hours and required the contribution of over 100 specialists.

---

5. The first antibiotic discovered: penicillin

- **Details:** In 1928, Alexander Fleming discovered penicillin, the world's first antibiotic.
- **Place:** United Kingdom.
- **Curiosity:** This discovery revolutionized the treatment of bacterial infections.

---

6. Longest successful resuscitation: Audrey Schoeman

- **Details:** After a 6-hour cardiac arrest, Audrey was successfully resuscitated.
- **Place:** Spain.
- **Curiosity:** Hypothermia protected his organs, allowing for a full recovery.

---

7. Largest epidemic contained: Ebola

- **Details:** In 2014, a global effort contained an epidemic that affected more than 28,000 people in West Africa.
- **Place:** West Africa.
- **Curiosity:** Vaccines and health protocols have played a crucial role in managing the epidemic.

---

8. The longest separation of conjoined twins: Jadon and Anias McDonald

- **Details:** The operation to separate the twins joined at the head lasted 27 hours.
- **Place:** United States.
- **Curiosity:** The surgery involved a multidisciplinary team of over 40 doctors.

---

9. The discovery of the structure of DNA: Watson and Crick

- **Details:** In 1953, they described the double helix structure of DNA.
- **Place:** United Kingdom.
- **Curiosity:** This discovery laid the foundation for modern genetics and personalized medicine.

10. Largest multiple transplant: 6 organs

- **Details:** One patient received the stomach, liver, pancreas, small intestine, large intestine and kidneys in one operation.
- **Place:** United States.
- **Curiosity:** The surgery required over 20 hours of surgical work.

11. The first CRISPR treatment: sickle cell disease

- **Details:** In 2019, a patient with sickle cell disease was successfully treated using the CRISPR gene editing technique.
- **Place:** United States.
- **Curiosity:** This approach has opened up new possibilities for the treatment of genetic diseases.

12. The longest anesthesia in suspension state: Erika Nordby

- **Details:** Erika, a Canadian girl, survived after being in a state of cryogenic suspension for 2 hours.
- **Place:** Canada.
- **Curiosity:** The cold protected his brain, preventing permanent damage.

13. Most corneal transplants in one day: 1,000

- **Details:** An Indian medical team completed 1,000 cornea transplants in 24 hours.
- **Place:** India.
- **Curiosity:** This mass intervention was organized to combat blindness in a rural region.

---

14. The first permanent artificial heart machine: Jarvik-7

- **Details:** This device was first implanted in 1982.
- **Place:** United States.
- **Curiosity:** While not perfect, the Jarvik-7 represented a milestone in cardiology.

---

15. The largest vaccination campaign: polio

- **Details:** The World Health Organization has vaccinated more than 2.5 billion children against polio.
- **Place:** Global.
- **Curiosity:** Thanks to this campaign, polio was almost completely eradicated.

---

16. The first open heart surgery: Ludwig Rehn

- **Details:** In 1896, Rehn performed the first open-heart surgery to suture a wound in the right ventricle.
- **Place:** Germany.
- **Curiosity:** The intervention was considered revolutionary for its time.

---

17. The longest chain of kidney donations: 35

- **Details:** A chain of 35 kidney transplants was completed in 2015 thanks to anonymous donors.
- **Place:** United States.

- **Curiosity:** This series of transplants was made possible thanks to an advanced matching system.

---

18. The discovery of the vaccine against COVID-19: BioNTech and Pfizer

- **Details:** In 2020, the first mRNA-based vaccine against COVID-19 was developed.
- **Place:** Germany/USA.
- **Curiosity:** The vaccine was developed in record time, less than a year after the virus was identified.

---

19. The largest number of organs transplanted from a single donor: 8

- **Details:** A deceased donor provided a heart, liver, kidney, lung, pancreas and intestine to several patients.
- **Place:** United States.
- **Curiosity:** This donation saved the lives of 8 people.

---

20. Largest collection of genetic data: Human Genome Project

- **Details:** Completed in 2003, it mapped the entire human genome.
- **Place:** Global.
- **Curiosity:** This scientific feat revolutionized medicine, paving the way for precision genetics.

Medicine never stops evolving, continually pushing the limits of imagination to save lives and improve human well-being. Each record is an example of how medical science can change the course of history.

4.2.3 Biotechnology and Genetics

Biotechnology and genetics represent some of the most innovative and transformative fields of modern science. Thanks to advanced techniques and an ever deeper understanding of DNA, humanity is able to modify living organisms for beneficial purposes, from medicine to agriculture, from energy to sustainability. Here are 20 extraordinary records that show the incredible potential of these disciplines.

---

1. The first human genome sequenced: Human Genome Project

- **Details:** Completed in 2003, it mapped the entire human genome, consisting of over 3 billion bases.
- **Place:** Global.
- **Curiosity:** This undertaking took 13 years and involved scientists from all over the world.

---

2. Largest genetic database: UK Biobank

- **Details:** It contains the genetic data of over 500,000 people.
- **Place:** United Kingdom.
- **Curiosity:** This resource is used to study genetic diseases and develop new therapies.

---

3. The first genetically modified organism: Escherichia coli bacterium

- **Details:** In 1973, scientists Herbert Boyer and Stanley Cohen created the first genetically modified bacterium.
- **Place:** United States.
- **Curiosity:** This experiment paved the way for modern genetic engineering.

---

4. **The most widely cultivated genetically modified plant: soybean**

- **Details:** Genetically modified soybeans cover more than 60% of the global cultivated area.
- **Place:** Global.
- **Curiosity:** Genetic modifications make the plant more resistant to pests and herbicides.

---

5. **The first cloned animal: Dolly the sheep**

- **Details:** Created in 1996, Dolly was the first mammal successfully cloned from an adult cell.
- **Place:** United Kingdom.
- **Curiosity:** Its birth revolutionized the debate on cloning and scientific ethics.

---

6. **The first genetically modified human embryo: CRISPR**

- **Details:** In 2015, Chinese researchers used CRISPR technology to edit a human embryo.
- **Place:** China.
- **Curiosity:** The experiment raised important ethical questions about gene editing.

---

7. **The longest synthetic DNA sequence: Mycoplasma mycoides**

- **Details:** Scientists have created an entire synthetic genome of 1.08 million bases.
- **Place:** United States.
- **Curiosity:** This genome was inserted into a bacterial cell, creating the first synthetic organism.

---

8. The largest genetic map of living species: Earth BioGenome Project

- **Details:** It aims to sequence the genomes of all 1.5 million known species on Earth.
- **Place:** Global.
- **Curiosity:** The project aims to preserve biodiversity and discover new biological applications.

---

9. The first drug produced from a genetically modified plant: Elelyso

- **Details:** Produced from GM tobacco, it is used to treat Gaucher disease.
- **Place:** United States.
- **Curiosity:** This innovation reduced pharmaceutical production costs.

---

10. The greatest genetic manipulation of a crop: Golden Rice

- **Details:** Rice has been enriched with beta-carotene to combat vitamin A deficiency.
- **Place:** Philippines.
- **Curiosity:** It was developed to reduce blindness in children in poor regions.

---

11. Fastest animal cloning: 10 piglets

- **Details:** In less than 60 days, a Chinese laboratory cloned 10 piglets using a robot.
- **Place:** China.
- **Curiosity:** This technology aims to improve the production of animals for research and agriculture.

---

12. The first gene therapy approved: Strimvelis

- **Details:** Used to treat severe combined immunodeficiency (ADA-SCID).
- **Place:** Europe.
- **Curiosity:** This therapy treats patients using genetically modified cells.

---

13. The first genetically modified fish: GloFish

- **Details:** This fluorescent fish was created for research purposes and marketed as a pet.
- **Place:** United States.
- **Curiosity:** Its characteristics make it a symbol of accessible biotechnology.

---

14. The first mRNA-based vaccine: Comirnaty

- **Details:** Developed by BioNTech and Pfizer, it was the first vaccine to use mRNA to fight COVID-19.
- **Place:** Germany/USA.
- **Curiosity:** mRNA technology opens up possibilities for treating many other diseases.

---

15. Largest bioethanol production: United States

- **Details:** In 2022, they produced 15.4 billion gallons of bioethanol.
- **Place:** United States.
- **Curiosity:** This fuel is produced from crops genetically improved for efficiency.

---

16. The largest ancient DNA sequence: Woolly mammoth

- **Details:** Researchers have sequenced the DNA of a 1.2 million-year-old mammoth.
- **Place:** Siberia.
- **Curiosity:** This study could help bring extinct species back to life.

---

17. The first GMO organism released into the environment: Aedes aegypti mosquito

- **Details:** Modified to reduce transmission of dengue and other diseases.
- **Place:** Brazil.
- **Curiosity:** These mosquitoes are sterile, limiting their population.

---

18. The first genetically modified organism to clean up the environment: Pseudomonas bacterium

- **Details:** It was developed to degrade oil in the seas.
- **Place:** United States.
- **Curiosity:** This bacterium represents an innovation in environmental biotechnology.

---

19. Largest CRISPR network: 10,000 labs

- **Details:** These labs collaborate to develop gene editing applications.
- **Place:** Global.
- **Curiosity:** The coordination accelerates research into genetic diseases and agricultural applications.

---

20. The first de-extinction project: Woolly mammoth

- **Details:** Researchers are trying to bring the woolly mammoth back to life by combining ancient and modern DNA.
- **Place:** United States.
- **Curiosity:** The project aims to repopulate tundra ecosystems with similar species.

Biotechnology and genetics continue to transform our understanding of life, offering innovative solutions to complex problems and opening new frontiers for the future of science and humanity.

5. Art and Culture

Introduction

Art and culture are the deepest expressions of human creativity. Through music, painting, literature, cinema and other artistic forms, humanity has celebrated beauty, explored emotions and shared stories that define our identity. This section explores the most extraordinary and surprising records achieved in the world of art and culture, demonstrating how creative ingenuity knows no boundaries.

5.1 Music

Introduction

Music is a universal language that unites people of all cultures, crossing linguistic and temporal barriers. From the evolution of musical instruments to breathtaking performances, music has always pushed the limits of human creativity. In this section, we celebrate records that demonstrate how rhythm, melody and harmony can reach incredible heights. From epic concerts to extraordinary compositions, let's discover together the most exceptional achievements in the world of music.

5.1.1 Record-Breaking Albums and Artists

Music is not just melody and harmony, but also a cultural phenomenon that inspires and unites generations. Albums and artists who achieve extraordinary milestones not only influence the music scene, but define moments in global cultural history. Below, 20 records that tell the lasting impact of artists and albums that made history.

---

1. Best-selling album of all time: *Thriller* on Michael Jackson

- **Details:** It has sold over 70 million copies worldwide.
- **Place:** Global.
- **Curiosity:** Includes legendary hits like *Billie Jean* and *Beat It*, who revolutionized the music industry.

---

2. Most streamed song: *Blinding Lights* by The Weeknd

- **Details:** It has exceeded 4 billion plays on Spotify.
- **Place:** Global.
- **Curiosity:** The single was a long-lasting phenomenon, remaining on the charts for over 90 weeks.

---

3. The artist with the most Grammys won: Beyoncé

- **Details:** He won 32 Grammys, surpassing the previous record.
- **Place:** United States.
- **Curiosity:** Beyoncé is recognized for her artistic versatility and breathtaking performances.

---

4. Best-selling album in a week: *25* by Adele

- **Details:** It sold 3.38 million copies in its first week in the United States.
- **Place:** Global.
- **Curiosity:** Adele has become a cultural icon thanks to her unique voice and emotional lyrics.

---

5. Highest-grossing music tour: *The Divide Tour* by Ed Sheeran

- **Details:** It grossed over $776 million.
- **Place:** Global.
- **Curiosity:** Ed Sheeran broke the previous record of *Rolling Stones*.

---

6. Fastest song to reach one billion views on YouTube: *Hello* by Adele

- **Details:** He reached the milestone in just 87 days.
- **Place:** Global.
- **Curiosity:** The video clip, directed by Xavier Dolan, contributed to the viral success of the song.

---

7. Most copies of an album sold on vinyl: *Abbey Road* day of the Beatles

- **Details:** It has sold over 10 million copies in vinyl format.
- **Place:** Global.
- **Curiosity:** The iconic cover of the group crossing the street has become a symbol of pop culture.

---

8. Youngest artist to reach number one: Billie Eilish

- **Details:** At 17, with the album *When We All Fall Asleep, Where Do We Go?*, reached the top of the charts.
- **Place:** Global.
- **Curiosity:** Billie is known for her unique style and deeply personal songs.

---

9. Best-selling single of all time: *White Christmas* on Bing Crosby

- **Details:** It has sold over 50 million copies.
- **Place:** Global.
- **Curiosity:** The song has become a timeless Christmas classic.

---

10. Artist with the most albums on the charts at one time: Prince

- **Details:** After his death, he placed 19 albums on the Billboard 200 chart.
- **Place:** United States.
- **Curiosity:** This record reflects the enormous cultural impact of his music.

---

11. The album with the most weeks on the charts: *The Dark Side of the Moon* dei Pink Floyd

- **Details:** It remained on the charts for over 950 weeks.
- **Place:** Global.
- **Curiosity:** It is considered one of the most influential albums in rock history.

---

12. The singer with the most gold records: Barbra Streisand

- **Details:** He received 52 gold records.
- **Place:** United States.

- **Curiosity:** Barbra is the only artist to achieve a number one album in six consecutive decades.

---

13. Most translated song: *Happy Birthday to You*

- **Details:** It has been translated into over 40 languages.
- **Place:** Global.
- **Curiosity:** The original melody dates back to 1893 and is universally recognized.

---

14. The most expensive album ever produced: *Invincible* on Michael Jackson

- **Details:** It had an estimated production cost of $30 million.
- **Place:** United States.
- **Curiosity:** Despite the high cost, the album received mixed reviews.

---

15. Most top 10 singles at one time: Drake

- **Details:** He placed 9 songs in the top 10 of the Billboard Hot 100 in just one week.
- **Place:** United States.
- **Curiosity:** Drake is a pioneer of the integration of rap and pop melodies.

---

16. The longest album: *69 Love Songs* dei Magnetic Fields

- **Details:** It lasts over 2 hours and 52 minutes, with 69 songs.
- **Place:** United States.
- **Curiosity:** The album is considered a masterpiece of irony and musical creativity.

---

17. Oldest artist to reach number one: Tony Bennett

- **Details:** At 85, he hit number one with his album *Duets II*.
- **Place:** United States.
- **Curiosity:** The album includes collaborations with artists such as Lady Gaga and Amy Winehouse.

---

18. The most listened to album on the day of release: *Midnights* di Taylor Swift

- **Details:** It totaled 184 million plays in 24 hours on Spotify.
- **Place:** Global.
- **Curiosity:** Taylor Swift continues to redefine musical success with each of her projects.

---

19. Longest #1 single: *Old Town Road* on Lil Nas

- **Details:** It remained atop the Billboard Hot 100 for 19 consecutive weeks.
- **Place:** United States.
- **Curiosity:** The collaboration with Billy Ray Cyrus made the song a cross-genre hit.

---

20. The concert with the largest audience: Rod Stewart

- **Details:** It attracted over 3.5 million people to Copacabana Beach in 1994.
- **Place:** Brazil.
- **Curiosity:** This free event is considered the largest concert in history.

These record-breaking albums and artists show how music is an art that spans time and space, influencing millions of people and leaving an indelible mark on global cultural history.

5.1.2 Concerts and Performances

Live music is one of the most powerful and engaging experiences that art can offer. Extraordinary concerts and performances have marked historic moments, attracting millions of spectators and setting records that celebrate the power of music to bring people together. Below, 20 unforgettable concert and performance records, with details of when and how they were achieved.

---

1. Greatest concert ever: Rod Stewart at Copacabana

- **Details:** It attracted over 3.5 million people.
- **Place and Date:** Copacabana Beach, Brazil, December 31, 1994.
- **Curiosity:** The free concert was organized to celebrate New Year's Eve and united generations in an unforgettable night.

---

2. Longest tour: U2's 360° Tour

- **Details:** It lasted 760 days, with 110 performances.
- **Place and Date:** Global, 2009 to 2011.
- **Curiosity:** With grosses of over $736 million, it was also one of the most profitable tours in history.

---

3. Highest performance at altitude: Metallica in Antarctica

- **Details:** They played in temperatures of -12°C to a limited audience of 120 people.
- **Place and Date:** Carlini Base, Antarctica, 8 December 2013.
- **Curiosity:** The performance was streamed, allowing fans around the world to watch.

---

4. The music festival with the largest number of spectators: Donauinselfest

- **Details:** It attracted around 3 million people.
- **Place and Date:** Danube Island, Vienna, Austria, 2015.
- **Curiosity:** This free event hosts artists from various genres and promotes European musical culture.

---

5. Longest Performance: Smokin' Joe McArthur

- **Details:** It played for 453 consecutive hours (18 days).
- **Place and Date:** United States, 1989.
- **Curiosity:** To meet the record, he could only take 5-minute breaks every hour.

---

6. The longest choral singing marathon: Hope Choir

- **Details:** The choir sang continuously for 101 hours.
- **Place and Date:** Rajasthan, India, 2017.
- **Curiosity:** The repertoire included songs in multiple languages, uniting different cultural traditions.

---

7. Most artists in a single concert: Live Aid

- **Details:** It involved more than 60 famous artists, including Queen, Elton John and David Bowie.
- **Place and Date:** London and Philadelphia, 13 July 1985.
- **Curiosity:** The event raised funds to fight famine in Ethiopia and is remembered as a milestone of live music.

---

8. Longest concert by a band: Flaming Lips

- **Details:** The band played for 24 hours straight.
- **Place and Date:** United States, 2012.

- **Curiosity:** The event was part of a project to break the record for consecutive performances in different cities.

---

9. The most expensive performance ever: Madonna at the Super Bowl

- **Details:** The estimated cost of production was $10 million.
- **Place and Date:** Indianapolis, USA, February 5, 2012.
- **Curiosity:** Madonna performed a 12-minute show with spectacular costumes and sets.

---

10. The largest number of paying spectators: Vasco Rossi at Modena Park

- **Details:** It attracted 225,173 paying spectators.
- **Place and Date:** Modena, Italy, 1 July 2017.
- **Curiosity:** This concert celebrated the 40 years of the Italian rocker's career.

---

11. Loudest Performance: Manowar

- **Details:** It reached 139 decibels during a concert.
- **Place and Date:** Hannover, Germania, 1994.
- **Curiosity:** Fans were asked to use ear protection during the show.

---

12. The longest concert ever recorded: Jazz Marathon

- **Details:** The musical marathon lasted 75 hours.
- **Place and Date:** New Orleans, USA, 1980.
- **Curiosity:** The event involved over 100 world-famous jazz musicians.

---

13. Greatest concert choreography: BTS

- **Details:** Over 50,000 fans participated in a synchronized choreography.
- **Place and Date:** Seoul, South Korea, 2021.
- **Curiosity:** The K-pop band is known for involving the audience in their shows.

---

14. Fastest performance at the North Pole: Katie Melua

- **Details:** He played in a nuclear submarine 300 meters below sea level.
- **Place and Date:** North Pole, October 1, 2006.
- **Curiosity:** This unique performance was organized to celebrate underwater technology.

---

15. The largest number of candles used during a concert: Andrea Bocelli

- **Details:** More than 10,000 candles illuminated the event.
- **Place and Date:** Florence, Italy, 2019.
- **Curiosity:** The concert combined classical music and an intimate and evocative atmosphere.

---

16. Longest concert at a single venue: Grateful Dead

- **Details:** They played for 5 hours straight.
- **Place and Date:** Cornell University, United States, May 8, 1977.
- **Curiosity:** This concert is considered one of the best in the band's history.

---

17. Largest symphony orchestra: National Music Arts Orchestra

- **Details:** It included 8,097 musicians.
- **Place and Date:** Franca, Brazil, 2013.
- **Curiosity:** The orchestra performed a repertoire of classical and popular music.

---

18. Most streamed concert: Travis Scott on Fortnite

- **Details:** It attracted over 12.3 million concurrent viewers.
- **Place and Date:** Online, April 23, 2020.
- **Curiosity:** This virtual event has revolutionized the way of conceiving concerts in the digital age.

---

19. The performance with the greatest number of lasers used: Jean-Michel Jarre

- **Details:** The show used over 100 synchronized lasers.
- **Place and Date:** Houston, USA, 5 April 1986.
- **Curiosity:** The event was a tribute to NASA astronauts.

---

20. Fastest concert organized after a tragedy: One Love Manchester

- **Details:** It was organized less than two weeks after the May 22, 2017 attack.
- **Place and Date:** Manchester, UK, 4 June 2017.
- **Curiosity:** Ariana Grande and other artists have raised over £17 million for victims.

These concerts and performances not only represent iconic moments in music history, but also demonstrate the power of music to inspire, unite and innovate.

5.1.3 Recording Musical Instruments

Musical instruments are the soul of music and have a long history of evolution, innovation and craftsmanship. Some instruments, due to their greatness, uniqueness or extraordinary capabilities, have set records that celebrate human creativity and the power of art. Below, 20 records linked to the most extraordinary musical instruments in the world.

---

1. The largest piano in the world: Challen Concert Grand

- **Details:** It measures 5.7 meters in length and weighs 1.25 tonnes.
- **Place:** United Kingdom.
- **Curiosity:** It was built for symphony concerts and is played on rare occasions.

---

2. The largest guitar in the world: Gibson Flying V

- **Details:** It is 13 meters long and fully functional.
- **Place:** Texas, United States.
- **Curiosity:** It was created by a group of students to promote music education.

---

3. The smallest violin in the world: David Edwards

- **Details:** It measures just 1.5cm in length.
- **Place:** United Kingdom.
- **Curiosity:** Despite its small size, it can be played with a tiny bow.

---

4. Largest pipe organ: Macy's Wanamaker Organ

- **Details:** It has 28,750 pipes and is 7 stories tall.
- **Place:** Philadelphia, United States.
- **Curiosity:** Live performances are performed every day inside Macy's department store.

---

5. The largest drum kit ever built: Mark Temperato

- **Details:** Includes over 813 pieces, including drums, cymbals and percussion.
- **Place:** United States.
- **Curiosity:** Mark uses this set for performances and educational workshops.

---

6. The longest harp in the world: Harp Pegasus

- **Details:** It measures 3.5 meters high.
- **Place:** Germany.
- **Curiosity:** The sound of this harp is so powerful that it can be heard 200 meters away.

---

7. The tallest trumpet ever built: Guinness Trombone

- **Details:** It is 32 meters tall and fully functional.
- **Place:** Swiss.
- **Curiosity:** Requires a team of three to play properly.

---

8. The oldest musical instrument ever found: Divje Babe Flute

- **Details:** Made from bear bone, it dates back 40,000 years.
- **Place:** Slovenia.
- **Curiosity:** It is considered one of the first examples of human creativity.

---

9. The most expensive guitar ever sold: David Gilmour's Black Strat

- **Details:** Sold for $3.9 million.
- **Place:** New York Auction, 2019.
- **Curiosity:** The proceeds were donated to climate charity.

---

10. The oldest functioning church organ: Basilica di Valère

- **Details:** It dates back to 1435 and is still used for concerts.
- **Place:** Swiss.
- **Curiosity:** It has a unique tone thanks to the original materials remaining intact.

---

11. Biggest Drum: Taiko Drums by Asano Taiko

- **Details:** It has a diameter of 3 meters.
- **Place:** Japan.
- **Curiosity:** It is played during traditional ceremonies and festivals.

---

12. The longest clarinet: Ivan Ivanovich

- **Details:** It is 2.1 meters long and produces deep, resonant notes.
- **Place:** Russia.
- **Curiosity:** It was designed to experiment with new tones in orchestral music.

---

13. The oldest working piano: Cristofori Piano

- **Details:** Built in 1720 by Bartolomeo Cristofori, the inventor of the piano.
- **Place:** Italy.

- **Curiosity:** It is preserved at the Museum of Musical Instruments in Florence.

---

14. The heaviest electric guitar: Rock Ock

- **Details:** It weighs over 400kg and has eight handles.
- **Place:** United Kingdom.
- **Curiosity:** It was built for a promotional campaign and requires multiple musicians to play.

---

15. Largest wind orchestra: Wuhan Philharmonic

- **Details:** It included 2,500 musicians who played together.
- **Place:** China.
- **Curiosity:** The event was organized to celebrate World Music Day.

---

16. The largest cello: Cello Monster

- **Details:** It is 5.5 meters tall.
- **Place:** Germany.
- **Curiosity:** To play it you need a stick-like instrument, used as a bow.

---

17. The longest xylophone in the world: Kyoto Forest Melody

- **Details:** It extends for 500 meters and was built in a forest.
- **Place:** Japan.
- **Curiosity:** The notes are activated by rolling a wooden ball along its surface.

---

18. The largest transverse flute: Flute Grandeur

- **Details:** It is 8 meters long.
- **Place:** India.
- **Curiosity:** It requires an entire team to control the air pressure and play a single note.

---

19. The heaviest musical instrument: Giant Marimba

- **Details:** It weighs 1.5 tons.
- **Place:** United States.
- **Curiosity:** Each bar produces a note that resonates for several minutes due to its amplitude.

---

20. The first digital instrument: Telharmonium

- **Details:** Built in 1897, it is considered the precursor of the synthesizer.
- **Place:** United States.
- **Curiosity:** It was so large that it took up an entire building and transmitted music over telephone lines.

Record-breaking musical instruments are not just objects, but symbols of humanity's mastery and innovation. Each instrument tells a unique story, pushing the boundaries of creativity and artistic expression.

5.2 Cinema

Introduction

Cinema is one of the most powerful and influential art forms in the world, capable of telling stories, exciting and inspiring viewers of every generation. From classic films that made history to TV series that define the modern era of streaming, cinema is an ever-evolving universe. In this section we explore the most surprising records related to films, TV series, directors and actors that have left an indelible mark on global culture.

5.2.1 Films and TV Series

The world of cinema and TV series has produced some of the most iconic works in the history of entertainment. From films that have broken box office records to series that have dominated streaming platforms, here are 20 extraordinary records related to these mediums of visual storytelling.

1. The highest-grossing film of all time: *Avatar*

- **Details:** It grossed over $2.9 billion.
- **Place and Date:** Global, 2009.
- **Curiosity:** Directed by James Cameron, it is famous for the innovative use of 3D technology.

2. The most expensive TV series ever produced: *The Lord of the Rings: The Rings of Power*

- **Details:** Each season has an estimated cost of $465 million.
- **Place and Date:** Global, 2022.
- **Curiosity:** It is based on the works of J.R.R. Tolkien and represents Amazon Prime Video's most ambitious investment.

3. The most awarded film at the Oscars: *The Lord of the Rings - The Return of the King*

- **Details:** He won 11 Oscars.
- **Place and Date:** United States, 2004.

- **Curiosity:** Shares the record with *Ben-How* and *Titanic.*

---

4. The longest series ever: *The Simpsons*

- **Details:** It has exceeded 750 episodes.
- **Place and Date:** United States, 1989 to present.
- **Curiosity:** *The Simpsons* is a pop culture icon, known for his satire and accurate predictions.

---

5. The most expensive film ever produced: *Pirates of the Caribbean: On Stranger Tides*

- **Details:** It had a budget of $379 million.
- **Place and Date:** Global, 2011.
- **Curiosity:** Much of the budget was spent on special effects and exotic locations.

---

6. The most watched TV series in streaming: *Stranger Things*

- **Details:** Season four amassed over 1.35 billion hours of viewership in its first 28 weeks.
- **Place and Date:** Global, 2022.
- **Curiosity:** The series is known for its '80s aesthetic and iconic soundtrack.

---

7. Highest-grossing film in an opening weekend: *Avengers: Endgame*

- **Details:** It grossed $1.2 billion in its first weekend.
- **Place and Date:** Global, 2019.
- **Curiosity:** This success was the culmination of over 20 films in the Marvel Cinematic Universe.

---

8. The most translated TV series: *Sesame Street*

- **Details:** It has been translated into over 140 languages.
- **Place and Date:** Global, since 1969.
- **Curiosity:** This educational program is known for its puppets and inclusive social themes.

---

9. The most expensive animated film: *Frozen II*

- **Details:** It had a budget of 150 million dollars.
- **Place and Date:** Global, 2019.
- **Curiosity:** The film grossed over $1.4 billion, becoming a modern classic.

---

10. Longest-running live-action TV series: *Doctor Who*

- **Details:** On the air since 1963, it has over 850 episodes.
- **Place and Date:** United Kingdom.
- **Curiosity:** It is famous for the concept of the protagonist, an alien capable of regenerating, which allowed the actors to be replaced without interrupting the plot.

---

11. Highest-grossing animated film: *The Lion King (2019)*

- **Details:** It grossed over $1.66 billion.
- **Place and Date:** Global, 2019.
- **Curiosity:** This CGI remake brought back the magic of the 1994 original.

---

12. Shortest TV series to win an Emmy: *Fleabag*

- **Details:** It won the Emmy for Best Comedy Series with only 12 episodes.
- **Place and Date:** United Kingdom, 2016-2019.

- **Curiosity:** Created by and starring Phoebe Waller-Bridge, it is one of the most critically acclaimed series.

---

13. The shortest film ever nominated for an Oscar: *Fresh Guacamole*

- **Details:** It lasts only 1 minute and 40 seconds.
- **Place and Date:** United States, 2012.
- **Curiosity:** It is an animated short film that uses stop-motion techniques.

---

14. Most Expensive Series Per Episode: *Game of Thrones*

- **Details:** Each episode of the eighth season cost approximately $15 million.
- **Place and Date:** Global, 2019.
- **Curiosity:** The high budgets were used for spectacular battles and visual effects.

---

15. Most Sequels: *Godzilla*

- **Details:** It has over 30 sequels since 1954.
- **Place and Date:** Japan/Global.
- **Curiosity:** Godzilla is a symbol of Japanese film culture and global science fiction.

---

16. The TV series with the highest number of live viewers: *MASH*

- **Details:** The final episode was watched by over 106 million viewers in the United States.
- **Place and Date:** United States, February 28, 1983.
- **Curiosity:** This episode still holds the record for American television.

17. Highest-grossing foreign film: *Parasite*

- **Details:** It grossed over $258 million.
- **Place and Date:** South Korea/Global, 2019.
- **Curiosity:** It is the first non-English language film to win the Oscar for Best Film.

18. The series with the highest number of Emmy awards: *Saturday Night Live*

- **Details:** He has won over 80 Emmys.
- **Place and Date:** United States, since 1975.
- **Curiosity:** This comedy show launched the careers of numerous actors and comedians.

19. The most watched film streamed in the first month: *Red Notice*

- **Details:** It totaled 364 million hours of viewing in its first month.
- **Place and Date:** Global, 2021.
- **Curiosity:** Starring Dwayne Johnson, Gal Gadot and Ryan Reynolds, it was a huge hit for Netflix.

20. Most locations used for a film: *The Lord of the Rings: The Trilogy*

- **Details:** Over 150 locations across New Zealand were used.
- **Place and Date:** New Zealand, 2001-2003.
- **Curiosity:** The spectacular natural settings contributed to the trilogy's epic appeal.

These records highlight the extraordinary impact of cinema and TV series on the world of culture and entertainment, celebrating the talent and passion of those who made them possible.

5.2.2 Revenues and Prizes

In the world of cinema, box office receipts and awards represent two of the main indicators of success. The takings show the public's appreciation, while the prizes recognize the artistic and technical value of a work. Some films and TV series have achieved exceptional results, setting records that remain etched in the history of entertainment. Here are 20 records linked to box office receipts and awards that have defined the cinema and television landscape.

---

1. The highest-grossing film globally ever: *Avatar*

- **Details:** It reached $2.9 billion at the box office.
- **Place and Date:** Global, 2009.
- **Curiosity:** Director James Cameron also holds second place with *Titanic.*

---

2. The highest-grossing animated film: *The Lion King* (2019)

- **Details:** It surpassed $1.66 billion.
- **Place and Date:** Global, 2019.
- **Curiosity:** It is a CGI remake of the 1994 Disney classic.

---

3. Highest grossing Marvel movie: *Avengers: Endgame*

- **Details:** It grossed $2.79 billion.
- **Place and Date:** Global, 2019.
- **Curiosity:** It was the most anticipated film of the modern era, with an epic conclusion for Marvel's characters.

4. The most expensive TV series ever: *The Lord of the Rings: The Rings of Power*

- **Details:** Each season costs approximately $465 million.
- **Place and Date:** Global, 2022.
- **Curiosity:** Amazon has invested record amounts to create a spectacular visual universe.

5. Highest-grossing film in its opening weekend: *Avengers: Endgame*

- **Details:** It grossed $1.2 billion in its first three days.
- **Place and Date:** Global, 2019.
- **Curiosity:** The film broke the previous record of *Avengers: Infinity War.*

6. The most awarded film in Oscar history: *The Lord of the Rings - The Return of the King*

- **Details:** He won 11 Oscars.
- **Place and Date:** United States, 2004.
- **Curiosity:** It won in every category in which it was nominated.

7. Highest-grossing foreign film: *Parasite*

- **Details:** He earned over $258 million.
- **Place and Date:** Global, 2019.
- **Curiosity:** It is the first non-English language film to win the Oscar for Best Film.

8. The most watched TV series ever: *Game of Thrones*

- **Details:** The finale attracted over 19 million viewers in the United States.
- **Place and Date:** Global, 2019.
- **Curiosity:** The series has spawned a global phenomenon with millions of fans.

---

9. Most Oscar statuettes won by a single film: *Ben-How*, *Titanic*, *The Lord of the Rings - The Return of the King*

- **Details:** Each of these films won 11 Oscars.
- **Place and Date:** United States, various years.
- **Curiosity:** These films represent cinematic milestones for their epic productions.

---

10. The most prestigious film festival: Cannes Film Festival

- **Details:** Every year it awards the best film with the Palme d'Or.
- **Place and Date:** France, since 1946.
- **Curiosity:** He is known for his artistic rigor and for promoting emerging talents.

---

11. The highest grossing domestic film in the United States: *Star Wars: The Force Awakens*

- **Details:** It grossed $936 million in the US.
- **Place and Date:** United States, 2015.
- **Curiosity:** It was the first chapter of the new trilogy of *Star Wars*.

---

12. The most awarded film at the Golden Globes: *La La Land*

- **Details:** It won 7 Golden Globes, including Best Film and Best Director.

- **Place and Date:** United States, 2017.
- **Curiosity:** The film celebrated the musical with a modern twist.

---

13. Highest grossing horror film ever: *It* (2017)

- **Details:** It grossed over $700 million.
- **Place and Date:** Global, 2017.
- **Curiosity:** Based on the novel by Stephen King, it redefined the horror genre.

---

14. The series with the most Emmys won: *Game of Thrones*

- **Details:** He won 59 Emmys.
- **Place and Date:** United States, 2011 to 2019.
- **Curiosity:** The series has become a global cultural phenomenon.

---

15. Highest-grossing animated film in a single day: *Frozen II*

- **Details:** It grossed $68 million in a single day.
- **Place and Date:** Global, 2019.
- **Curiosity:** The sequel consolidated the success of the Disney saga.

---

16. Highest-grossing film for a documentary: *Fahrenheit 9/11*

- **Details:** It grossed over $222 million.
- **Place and Date:** Global, 2004.
- **Curiosity:** Directed by Michael Moore, it explores political themes related to the events of 9/11.

---

17. Most Expensive Series Per Episode: *Game of Thrones*

- **Details:** Each episode of the eighth season cost 15 million dollars.
- **Place and Date:** Global, 2019.
- **Curiosity:** The battles and visual effects required unprecedented investment.

---

18. Highest grossing independent film: *The Blair Witch Project*

- **Details:** It grossed $248 million on a budget of just $60,000.
- **Place and Date:** Global, 1999.
- **Curiosity:** It was one of the first films promoted through viral marketing.

---

19. The highest-grossing film in the musical genre: *Bohemian Rhapsody*

- **Details:** It grossed over $905 million.
- **Place and Date:** Global, 2018.
- **Curiosity:** It tells the story of Freddie Mercury and Queen.

---

20. The oldest film award: Academy Award

- **Details:** The first ceremony was held on May 16, 1929.
- **Place and Date:** United States.
- **Curiosity:** The Oscars are the most coveted award in the world of cinema today.

These records show how box office receipts and awards are not only a recognition of the art of cinema, but also a testament to the impact that films and TV series can have on a global scale.

5.2.3 Record-breaking Actors and Directors

The world of cinema wouldn't be the same without the people who bring it to life: actors and directors. Some have left an indelible mark, setting incredible records through their talent, dedication and ability to captivate audiences. Here are 20 records linked to the actors and directors who redefined the history of cinema.

---

1. The actor with the most Oscars won: Daniel Day-Lewis

- **Details:** He won three Oscars for Best Actor for *My left foot* (1990), *The oilman* (2008) and *Lincoln* (2013).
- **Place and Date:** United States.
- **Curiosity:** He is known for his intense preparation for roles, often getting completely into character.

---

2. The actress with the most Oscars won: Katharine Hepburn

- **Details:** She won four Oscars for Best Actress.
- **Place and Date:** United States, between 1934 and 1982.
- **Curiosity:** Hepburn is recognized as one of the most influential figures of classic Hollywood cinema.

---

3. The director with the most Oscars won: John Ford

- **Details:** He won four Oscars for Best Director.
- **Place and Date:** United States.
- **Curiosity:** He is famous for his western films, such as *Red shadows* and *Wild trails*.

---

4. The actor with the most films shot: Eric Roberts

- **Details:** He has acted in over 600 films and television projects.
- **Place and Date:** United States, in business since 1978.
- **Curiosity:** Roberts is a ubiquitous face in B-movies and independent productions.

---

5. Highest paid actress for a single film: Scarlett Johansson

- **Details:** He earned $20 million for *Black Widow* (2021).
- **Place and Date:** United States.
- **Curiosity:** Scarlett is one of the most influential actresses in the Marvel Cinematic Universe.

---

6. Highest paid director for a single film: Christopher Nolan

- **Details:** He earned $100 million for *Tenet* (2020), between fees and percentages of proceeds.
- **Place and Date:** Global.
- **Curiosity:** Nolan is known for his complex and visually spectacular narratives.

---

7. Youngest actor to win an Oscar: Tatum O'Neal

- **Details:** He won the Oscar at 10 years old *Paper Moon* (1974).
- **Place and Date:** United States.
- **Curiosity:** She remains the youngest winner in Oscar history.

---

8. Youngest director to win an Oscar: Damien Chazelle

- **Details:** He won the Oscar for Best Director at 32 for *La La Land* (2017).
- **Place and Date:** United States.

- **Curiosity:** Chazelle is known for his love of music and emotional stories.

---

9. The highest grossing actor globally: Samuel L. Jackson

- **Details:** The films he starred in have grossed over $27 billion.
- **Place and Date:** Global.
- **Curiosity:** He is an icon of action cinema and a familiar face in Marvel films.

---

10. Oldest actor to win an Oscar: Anthony Hopkins

- **Details:** He won the Oscar at 83 for *The Father* (2021).
- **Place and Date:** United States.
- **Curiosity:** Hopkins surprised the world with his moving performance.

---

11. Director with the most films on the Top 100 list: Steven Spielberg

- **Details:** He directed 5 films listed by the American Film Institute.
- **Place and Date:** United States.
- **Curiosity:** Spielberg is a legend of cinema, author of classics such as *E.T.* and *Jurassic Park*.

---

12. The actress with the longest career: Marsha Hunt

- **Details:** He had a career that spanned over 80 years.
- **Place and Date:** United States.
- **Curiosity:** Hunt was an important figure both in front of and behind the scenes in Hollywood.

---

13. The actor with the most physical transformation: Christian Bale

- **Details:** He lost 28 kg for *The sleepless man* (2004) and gained 20 kg per *Vice* (2018).
- **Place and Date:** United States.
- **Curiosity:** Bale is famous for his physical and mental commitment to roles.

---

14. The actor with the most Oscar nominations: Jack Nicholson

- **Details:** He received 12 nominations throughout his career.
- **Place and Date:** United States.
- **Curiosity:** Nicholson is known for his iconic roles in films such as *One Flew Over the Cuckoo's Nest.*

---

15. Highest-grossing director globally for a single film: James Cameron

- **Details:** With *Avatar*, reached $2.9 billion.
- **Place and Date:** Global, 2009.
- **Curiosity:** Cameron revolutionized cinema with innovative technologies.

---

16. Actor with the most diverse roles: Lon Chaney

- **Details:** He was known as "the man of a thousand faces" for his ability to transform.
- **Place and Date:** United States, 1920s.
- **Curiosity:** He is a legend of silent cinema and horror.

---

17. Highest-grossing female director: Patty Jenkins

- **Details:** *Wonder Woman* it grossed $822 million.

- **Place and Date:** Global, 2017.
- **Curiosity:** Patty Jenkins was a point of reference for women in action cinema.

18. Actor with the most action scenes: Jackie Chan

- **Details:** He has performed over 10,000 action sequences without stunt doubles.
- **Place and Date:** Global.
- **Curiosity:** Jackie Chan is famous for his extreme stunts and unique humor.

19. The director with the longest average film length: Andrei Tarkovsky

- **Details:** His films have an average duration of over 2.5 hours.
- **Place and Date:** Russia.
- **Curiosity:** Tarkovsky is celebrated for his philosophical and visually poetic approach.

20. Actor with the most dubbed roles: Mel Blanc

- **Details:** He has voiced over 400 characters, including Bugs Bunny and Daffy Duck.
- **Place and Date:** United States.
- **Curiosity:** He is known as "the man of a thousand voices" for his incredible versatility.

These records demonstrate how actors and directors have contributed to making cinema an immortal art form, achieving unique goals and inspiring generations of viewers and creators.

5.3 Literature

Introduction

Literature is the cradle of imagination and knowledge. Through books, humanity has told stories, transmitted culture and challenged the boundaries of the mind. From classics that have spanned the centuries to modern bestsellers, literature continues to inspire and connect people. In this section we explore the most incredible records related to books, authors and literary works that have left a lasting imprint on the history of writing.

5.3.1 Book and Author

Books and their authors have marked eras and cultures, setting surprising records for sales, translations, speed of writing and cultural impact. Below, 20 records related to the world of literature.

1. Best-selling book of all time: The Bible

- **Details:** It is estimated that over 5 billion copies have been distributed.
- **Place:** Global.
- **Curiosity:** It has been translated into over 3,000 languages, making it accessible to almost the entire world's population.

2. Best-selling novel: *Don Quixote* by Miguel de Cervantes

- **Details:** It has sold over 500 million copies.
- **Place:** Spain/global.
- **Curiosity:** Published in 1605, it is considered one of the masterpieces of world literature.

3. Best-selling book series: *Harry Potter* at J.K. Rowling

- **Details:** It has sold over 500 million copies worldwide.
- **Place:** Global.
- **Curiosity:** The series introduced millions of young people to reading, transforming the writer into one of the richest authors in the world.

---

4. The most translated book: *The Adventures of Pinocchio* by Carlo Collodi

- **Details:** Translated into over 300 languages and dialects.
- **Place:** Italy/global.
- **Curiosity:** The story of the wooden puppet has enchanted generations of readers.

---

5. The book with the highest number of copies sold in 24 hours: *Harry Potter and the Deathly Hallows*

- **Details:** It sold 8.3 million copies in its first 24 hours.
- **Place:** Global, 2007.
- **Curiosity:** This record has consecrated the saga as a cultural phenomenon.

---

6. The longest novel: *In search of lost time* by Marcel Proust

- **Details:** It includes 1.2 million words in seven volumes.
- **Place:** France.
- **Curiosity:** He is known for his long sentences and minute details that explore memory and time.

---

7. The most expensive book ever sold: *Codex Leicester* by Leonardo da Vinci

- **Details:** Sold for $30.8 million.
- **Place and Date:** Auction, United States, 1994.
- **Curiosity:** It was purchased by Bill Gates, who later digitized it to share with the public.

---

8. The most prolific author: Ryoki Inoue

- **Details:** He wrote over 1,000 novels.
- **Place:** Brazil.
- **Curiosity:** He is known for his ability to complete a book in a few days.

---

9. The Oldest Book: *Epic of Gilgamesh*

- **Details:** It dates back approximately 4,000 years.
- **Place:** Mesopotamia.
- **Curiosity:** It is one of the earliest examples of written literature, carved on clay tablets.

---

10. Youngest author to publish a bestseller: Dorothy Straight

- **Details:** He wrote *How the World Began* at the age of 4.
- **Place:** United States, 1964.
- **Curiosity:** The book was published with the help of his parents.

---

11. The shortest book ever published: *The Dinosaur* by Augusto Monterroso

- **Details:** Contains only 9 words.
- **Place:** Guatemala.
- **Curiosity:** Despite its brevity, it is considered a cornerstone of flash fiction.

12. The richest author in the world: J.K. Rowling

- **Details:** He has amassed a fortune of more than $1 billion from his book and film rights.
- **Place:** United Kingdom.
- **Curiosity:** Rowling wrote the first Harry Potter book during a time of economic difficulty.

---

13. The book with the most characters: *War and peace* by Leo Tolstoy

- **Details:** Includes over 500 characters.
- **Place:** Russia.
- **Curiosity:** The novel explores Russian society during the Napoleonic era.

---

14. The first printed book: *The Gutenberg Bible*

- **Details:** Printed in 1455 with the movable type printing technique.
- **Place:** Germany.
- **Curiosity:** It marked the beginning of the diffusion of books on a large scale.

---

15. Best-selling children's book: *The little prince* by Antoine de Saint-Exupéry

- **Details:** It has sold over 140 million copies.
- **Place:** France/global.
- **Curiosity:** It is one of the most translated books, with versions in over 300 languages.

16. The most read book after the Bible: *The Koran*

- **Details:** It is estimated that billions of copies have been read or acted.
- **Place:** Global.
- **Curiosity:** It is the sacred text of Islam, fundamental for millions of people.

---

17. Best-selling book in a single country: *Five steps in the dark* di Jin Yong

- **Details:** It has sold over 100 million copies in China.
- **Place:** China.
- **Curiosity:** Jin Yong is one of the most beloved authors in modern Chinese literature.

---

18. Best-selling science fiction book: *Dune* in Frank Herbert

- **Details:** It has sold over 20 million copies.
- **Place:** United States.
- **Curiosity:** It is considered a cornerstone of the science fiction genre.

---

19. The largest number of copies of a book donated: *The Arabian Nights*

- **Details:** Over 10 million copies have been donated by various governments to promote Arabic culture.
- **Place:** Middle East/Global.
- **Curiosity:** This collection of short stories has influenced many literary traditions.

---

20. The most stolen book in libraries: *The Guinness Book of Records*

- **Details:** It is the book most frequently removed from the shelves of public libraries.
- **Place:** Global.
- **Curiosity:** Its popularity makes it a target for record enthusiasts.

These records demonstrate how books and authors have had an extraordinary impact on society, leaving a legacy that continues to inspire readers of all ages.

5.3.2 Libraries and Bookshops

Libraries and bookshops are the temples of knowledge, custodians of thousands, sometimes millions, of volumes that tell the history of humanity. From ancient libraries that have preserved precious manuscripts to modern bookstores that celebrate reading, these places represent the beating heart of culture. Below, 20 extraordinary records linked to libraries and bookstores around the world.

---

1. The largest library in the world: Library of Congress

- **Details:** It contains over 170 million documents, including books, manuscripts and maps.
- **Place:** Washington D.C., United States.
- **Curiosity:** It was founded in 1800 and is also open to researchers from all over the world.

---

2. The world's largest bookstore: Barnes & Noble, Fifth Avenue

- **Details:** It has an area of over 14,000 m² and offers millions of books.
- **Place:** New York, United States.

- **Curiosity:** In addition to books, it hosts literary events and spaces dedicated to reading.

---

3. The oldest library still in use: Library of San Domenico

- **Details:** Founded in 1250, it has been active for over 770 years.
- **Place:** Bologna, Italy.
- **Curiosity:** It contains precious medieval manuscripts and historical documents.

---

4. The oldest bookshop still in business: Bertrand Livoltos

- **Details:** Founded in 1732, it has been in operation for almost 300 years.
- **Place:** Lisbon, Portugal.
- **Curiosity:** It is recognized by Guinness World Records as the oldest bookstore in the world.

---

5. Most popular library: New York Public Library

- **Details:** Every year it welcomes over 17 million visitors.
- **Place:** New York, United States.
- **Curiosity:** Its main reading room, the Rose Main Reading Room, is one of the most iconic places in the city.

---

6. The tallest library in the world: Zhongshuge Library

- **Details:** Located in a 52-story skyscraper.
- **Place:** Chongqing, Cina.
- **Curiosity:** Its futuristic design includes shelves that extend to the ceiling.

---

7. The most technological library: Bibliotheca Alexandrina

- **Details:** Equipped with a robotic system for retrieving books.
- **Place:** Alexandria, Egypt.
- **Curiosity:** It is a tribute to the historic Library of Alexandria of antiquity.

---

8. The most remote bookstore: Eterna Cadencia

- **Details:** Located in Chilean Patagonia, it serves an isolated community.
- **Place:** Chile.
- **Curiosity:** The books are transported by mule to reach the bookshop.

---

9. The library with the largest number of digital volumes: National Library of China

- **Details:** Contains over 5 million digital books.
- **Place:** Beijing, China.
- **Curiosity:** It is one of the major centers for the digitization of historical texts.

---

10. The most photographed bookshop in the world: Livraria Lello

- **Details:** With its ornate interior, it is considered one of the most beautiful libraries.
- **Place:** Porto, Portugal.
- **Curiosity:** It is said to have inspired J.K. Rowling for the creation of Hogwarts.

---

11. The quietest library: National Library of Finland

- **Details:** It was designed to guarantee perfect acoustics.

160

- **Place:** Helsinki, Finland.
- **Curiosity:** Visitors describe the place as a "temple of silence".

---

12. The smallest bookshop: Crosthwaite Bookshop

- **Details:** It measures just 3m² and holds 100 books.
- **Place:** United Kingdom.
- **Curiosity:** It serves a small rural community of a few hundred inhabitants.

---

13. The largest university library: Bodleian Library

- **Details:** Contains over 13 million volumes.
- **Place:** Oxford, UK.
- **Curiosity:** It is one of the UK's legal deposit libraries, receiving a copy of every book published.

---

14. The most colorful bookstore: Zhongshuge Rainbow Bookstore

- **Details:** Its interiors are decorated with multicolored shelves and mirrors that amplify the spaces.
- **Place:** Hangzhou, China.
- **Curiosity:** It is a tourist attraction as well as a reference point for readers.

---

15. The highest library: Admont Monastery Library

- **Details:** It has ceilings that reach 70 meters in height.
- **Place:** Austria.
- **Curiosity:** It is famous for its baroque frescoes and the natural light that illuminates the spaces.

16. The bookstore with the most titles: Powell's City of Books

- **Details:** Contains over 1 million titles available for sale.
- **Place:** Portland, United States.
- **Curiosity:** It spans an entire city block and is an icon for readers.

17. The largest floating library: Logos Hope

- **Details:** Contains over 5,000 titles.
- **Place:** Traveling ship, Global.
- **Curiosity:** He travels around the world to bring books to remote places.

18. The largest library built in a cave: Yunshuge Library

- **Details:** It is carved into the rock and houses thousands of volumes.
- **Place:** China.
- **Curiosity:** Its unique location attracts tourists and curious readers.

19. The library with the largest number of rare books: Vatican Library

- **Details:** It contains over 80,000 manuscripts and ancient texts.
- **Place:** Vatican City.
- **Curiosity:** Many documents are not accessible to the public, but are studied by specialized researchers.

20. The most extravagant bookstore: The Last Bookstore

- **Details:** Includes art installations made from old books.
- **Place:** Los Angeles, United States.
- **Curiosity:** In addition to being a bookshop, it is also an art gallery and event space.

These extraordinary places demonstrate how libraries and bookstores are much more than physical spaces: they are symbols of our thirst for knowledge, creativity and cultural connection.

5.3.3 Writing and Publication Records

Writing and publishing books are processes that combine creativity, discipline and innovation. Throughout history, authors, publishers, and even machines have set extraordinary records that demonstrate how the art of writing can surpass limits. Here are 20 fascinating records related to the world of writing and publishing.

---

1. The fastest written book: *The Boy in the Dress* on David Walliams

- **Details:** The author completed the book in just 24 hours.
- **Place and Date:** United Kingdom, 2008.
- **Curiosity:** Despite the record time, the book became a bestseller.

---

2. The longest book ever written in a single sitting: *Marathon Writing* by Deepak Sharma

- **Details:** The author wrote 250,000 words in 20 hours.
- **Place and Date:** India, 2018.
- **Curiosity:** Sharma used intense physical and mental preparation to take on the challenge.

3. Most books written in one year: Barbara Cartland

- **Details:** He wrote 23 novels in just one year.
- **Place and Date:** United Kingdom, 1983.
- **Curiosity:** Cartland is famous for her romance novels and her fast-paced writing style.

4. Book published fastest after being written: *Harry Potter and the Goblet of Fire*

- **Details:** It was published just 10 weeks after the manuscript was submitted.
- **Place and Date:** United Kingdom, 2000.
- **Curiosity:** The public's anticipation accelerated all phases of the publication.

5. The smallest book ever published: *Teeny Ted from Turnip Town*

- **Details:** It measures 70 x 100 micrometers, smaller than a grain of sand.
- **Place and Date:** Canada, 2007.
- **Curiosity:** The book is readable only with an electron microscope.

6. The longest writing ever completed by a single author: *Genpei's novel* di Eiji Yoshikawa

- **Details:** It includes over 15,000 pages.
- **Place:** Japan.
- **Curiosity:** The author dedicated decades to this monumental work.

7. The largest number of authors involved in a single book: *The Wisdom of Crowds*

- **Details:** Written by 5,000 different authors.
- **Place and Date:** Global, 2015.
- **Curiosity:** Each author contributed a sentence to the book.

---

8. Most books published in one day: Penguin Random House

- **Details:** It published 600 titles in 24 hours.
- **Place and Date:** Global, 2012.
- **Curiosity:** This event was organized to celebrate the 75th anniversary of the publishing house.

---

9. The largest book ever printed: *This is the Prophet Mohammed*

- **Details:** It measures 5 x 8.06 meters and weighs 1,500 kg.
- **Place and Date:** Dubai, United Arab Emirates, 2012.
- **Curiosity:** It contains a biography of the Prophet Muhammad and was created to promote Islamic culture.

---

10. The largest number of copies of a book printed in one day: *Harry Potter and the Half-Blood Prince*

- **Details:** 10.8 million copies printed in 24 hours.
- **Place and Date:** Global, 2005.
- **Curiosity:** Global demand for the book necessitated large-scale production.

---

11. The book written with the greatest digital speed: *One Second Novel*

- **Details:** Composed in a second thanks to an algorithm.
- **Place and Date:** Japan, 2019.

- **Curiosity:** The content was generated by artificial intelligence.

---

12. The book published in multiple editions: *The Little Prince* by Antoine de Saint-Exupéry

- **Details:** Available in over 15,000 different editions.
- **Place and Date:** Global, since 1943.
- **Curiosity:** Each edition features unique illustrations and different translations.

---

13. The oldest preserved manuscript: *The Pyramid Texts*

- **Details:** It dates back approximately 4,400 years.
- **Place:** Egypt.
- **Curiosity:** It is carved on the walls of the tombs of the pharaohs.

---

14. The published book with the most illustrations: *The Codex Atlanticus* by Leonardo da Vinci

- **Details:** Contains over 1,750 drawings.
- **Place:** Italy.
- **Curiosity:** It is a collection of notes, sketches and inventions of the Renaissance genius.

---

15. The book written in the most languages: *Earth* by Pico Iyer

- **Details:** Written in 200 languages.
- **Place and Date:** Global, 2017.
- **Curiosity:** Each chapter was written in a different language.

16. The book written in record time by a robot: *AI Writes Poetry*

- **Details:** Composed entirely by artificial intelligence in 15 minutes.
- **Place and Date:** United States, 2020.
- **Curiosity:** The poems are inspired by classical and modern literary styles.

---

17. Most self-published books: John Locke

- **Details:** He self-published 12 bestsellers in one year.
- **Place and Date:** United States, 2011.
- **Curiosity:** He was the first self-published author to sell a million copies on Kindle.

---

18. The fastest printed book: *One-Minute Press Book*

- **Details:** Printed in 60 seconds thanks to an advanced printer.
- **Place and Date:** Germany, 2018.
- **Curiosity:** The technology was developed to reduce production times.

---

19. Most pages in a picture book: *The Great Book of the World*

- **Details:** Includes 5,000 pages of illustrations.
- **Place and Date:** France, 2015.
- **Curiosity:** Each page represents a country with detailed images and text.

---

20. The manuscript written with the greatest calligraphic precision: *The Topkapi Quran*

- **Details:** Each letter is identical in size and style.

- **Place:** Türkiye.
- **Curiosity:** It is a masterpiece of Islamic writing and a cultural treasure.

These records demonstrate that writing and publishing are not just creative processes, but also extraordinary feats that push the limits of technology, innovation, and human dedication.

6. Sport

Introduction

Sport is a universal language that unites people of all ages, cultures and nations. Through competitions, individual and team exploits, sport celebrates human limits, courage and dedication. This section explores extraordinary records across disciplines, highlighting performances that have inspired millions of people around the world.

6.1 Athletics and Endurance

Introduction

Athletics and endurance-related disciplines represent the heart of sporting competitions. With roots dating back to ancient times, athletics has always challenged human limits in speed, strength and endurance. In this section, we celebrate legendary records in running, jumping and throwing competitions, where every millimeter and every fraction of a second counts.

6.1.1 Running, Jumping and Throwing

The disciplines of running, jumping and throwing are among the most iconic in athletics. These events not only measure physical strength and technique, but also the will to overcome one's limits.

Here are 20 extraordinary records achieved by athletes who have written the history of these disciplines.

1. Fastest 100m run: Usain Bolt

- **Details:** World record of 9.58 seconds.
- **Place and Date:** Berlin, Germany, 2009.
- **Curiosity:** His incredible acceleration earned him the nickname "The Fastest Man Alive".

2. Longest run without breaks: Dean Karnazes

- **Details:** He ran 560 km in 80 hours and 44 minutes without sleep.
- **Place and Date:** United States, 2005.
- **Curiosity:** Karnazes is known for his incredible feats of endurance.

3. Highest high jump: Javier Sotomayor

- **Details:** He jumped 2.45 meters.
- **Place and Date:** Salamanca, Spain, 1993.
- **Curiosity:** This record still stands, making it one of the most enduring in the history of athletics.

4. Longest long jump: Mike Powell

- **Details:** He jumped 8.95 meters.
- **Place and Date:** Tokyo, Japan, 1991.
- **Curiosity:** The record was set during a historic competition against Carl Lewis.

5. The farthest javelin throw: Jan Železný

- **Details:** He threw the javelin 98.48 meters.
- **Place and Date:** Jena, Germany, 1996.
- **Curiosity:** Železný is considered the greatest javelin thrower in history.

---

6. Fastest 200m run: Usain Bolt

- **Details:** World record of 19.19 seconds.
- **Place and Date:** Berlin, Germany, 2009.
- **Curiosity:** Bolt holds both the 100 and 200 meter records.

---

7. Longest triple jump: Jonathan Edwards

- **Details:** He jumped 18.29 meters.
- **Place and Date:** Gothenburg, Sweden, 1995.
- **Curiosity:** Edwards broke his own world record twice in the same competition.

---

8. Farthest shot put: Randy Barnes

- **Details:** He threw the shot put 23.12 meters.
- **Place and Date:** Los Angeles, United States, 1990.
- **Curiosity:** This record still stands after more than three decades.

---

9. Fastest marathon runner: Eliud Kipchoge

- **Details:** World record of 2 hours, 1 minute and 9 seconds.
- **Place and Date:** Berlin, Germany, 2022.
- **Curiosity:** Kipchoge is also known for being the first man to run a marathon under 2 hours (unofficial).

10. Highest pole vaulter: Armand Duplantis

- **Details:** It reached 6.21 meters.
- **Place and Date:** Eugene, United States, 2022.
- **Curiosity:** Duplantis has broken his own records multiple times, continuing to push the limits of the discipline.

11. Fastest 400m run: Wayde van Niekerk

- **Details:** World record of 43.03 seconds.
- **Place and Date:** Rio de Janeiro, Brazil, 2016.
- **Curiosity:** He set the record by running in the outermost lane, considered the most difficult.

12. The farthest discus throw: Jürgen Schult

- **Details:** He threw the discus 74.08 meters.
- **Place and Date:** Neubrandenburg, Germania, 1986.
- **Curiosity:** This record has stood for almost 40 years.

13. Highest standing jump: Kadour Ziani

- **Details:** He reached a height of 1.85 meters when standing still.
- **Place and Date:** France, 2001.
- **Curiosity:** Ziani is famous for his incredible skills as a basketball spiker.

14. Fastest 4x100 meter relay: Jamaica

- **Details:** World record of 36.84 seconds.
- **Place and Date:** London, UK, 2012.

- **Curiosity:** The team included Usain Bolt, Yohan Blake, Nesta Carter and Michael Frater.

---

15. Highest high jump for women: Stefka Kostadinova

- **Details:** He jumped 2.09 meters.
- **Place and Date:** Rome, Italy, 1987.
- **Curiosity:** This record has stood unbeaten for over three decades.

---

16. The longest long jump for women: Galina Chistyakova

- **Details:** He jumped 7.52 meters.
- **Place and Date:** Leningrad, Russia, 1988.
- **Curiosity:** Chistyakova is one of the most consistent athletes of her era.

---

17. The farthest hammer throw: Yuriy Sedykh

- **Details:** He threw the hammer 86.74 meters.
- **Place and Date:** Stuttgart, Germany, 1986.
- **Curiosity:** Sedykh has dominated this discipline for over a decade.

---

18. The longest run in a desert: Mauro Prosperi

- **Details:** He traveled over 300km in the Sahara after getting lost during the Marathon des Sables.
- **Place and Date:** Morocco, 1994.
- **Curiosity:** Prosperi survived thanks to extraordinary willpower and ingenuity.

19. Fastest 1500m run: Hicham El Guerrouj

- **Details:** World record of 3 minutes and 26 seconds.
- **Place and Date:** Rome, Italy, 1998.
- **Curiosity:** El Guerrouj is considered one of the best middle distance runners ever.

---

20. Most Olympic medals in athletics: Paavo Nurmi

- **Details:** He won 12 Olympic medals, including 9 gold.
- **Place and Date:** Various editions, 1920-1928.
- **Curiosity:** Nurmi, nicknamed "The Flying Finn", is an athletics legend.

These records represent the best of athletics and show how determination, talent and hard work can lead to extraordinary results.

6.1.2 Water Sports

Water sports combine physical and mental skills to tackle one of the most powerful elements: water. From Olympic swimming pools to the open oceans, these records demonstrate how athletes have pushed the limits of endurance, speed and creativity. Below, 20 extraordinary records celebrating feats in swimming, diving, rowing and other aquatic disciplines.

---

1. Fastest swim in the 100 meter freestyle: César Cielo

- **Details:** World record of 46.91 seconds.
- **Place and Date:** Rome, Italy, 2009.
- **Curiosity:** Cielo is considered one of the greatest swimmers in the history of freestyle.

---

2. Most Olympic medals in swimming: Michael Phelps

- **Details:** He won 28 Olympic medals, including 23 gold.
- **Place and Date:** Various editions, 2004-2016.
- **Curiosity:** Phelps is known as "The Baltimore Cannibal" for his dominance in swimming pools.

---

3. Longest swim: Chloe McCardel

- **Details:** He swam 124.4km non-stop.
- **Place and Date:** Bahamas, 2014.
- **Curiosity:** McCardel challenged physical and mental limits in challenging ocean conditions.

---

4. Most dives in one day: Ahmed Gabr

- **Details:** He completed 100 dives in 24 hours.
- **Place and Date:** Red Sea, Egypt, 2015.
- **Curiosity:** Gabr has shown incredible physical and mental resilience to reach this milestone.

---

5. Fastest swim in the 50 meter breaststroke: Adam Peaty

- **Details:** World record of 25.95 seconds.
- **Place and Date:** Gwangju, Corea del Sud, 2019.
- **Curiosity:** Peaty is known for revolutionizing breaststroke with his innovative technique.

---

6. Fastest crossing of the English Channel: Trent Grimsey

- **Details:** He completed the crossing in 6 hours and 55 minutes.
- **Place and Date:** English Channel, UK-France, 2012.

- **Curiosity:** Grimsey braved freezing waters and challenging currents.

---

7. Longest rowing race: Atlantic Row Challenge

- **Details:** It covers 4,800 km across the Atlantic Ocean.
- **Place and Date:** From La Gomera (Spain) to Antigua, every year.
- **Curiosity:** The challenge is known for pushing participants to the limit of their endurance.

---

8. Most world records in swimming: Michael Phelps

- **Details:** He held 39 world records during his career.
- **Place and Date:** Global.
- **Curiosity:** Phelps dominated in multiple disciplines, from freestyle to butterfly.

---

9. The longest freedive underwater: Aleix Segura

- **Details:** He held his breath for 24 minutes and 3 seconds.
- **Place and Date:** Barcelona, Spain, 2016.
- **Curiosity:** Segura used advanced oxygenation techniques to prepare.

---

10. The kayak speed record: Ken Wallace

- **Details:** It reached a speed of 25 km/h in calm waters.
- **Place and Date:** Australia, 2018.
- **Curiosity:** Wallace is an Olympic champion in sprint kayaking.

---

11. The longest rowing crossing: Fedor Konyukhov

- **Details:** It crossed the Pacific Ocean, covering 16,500 km.
- **Place and Date:** Australia-Chile, 2013.
- **Curiosity:** Konyukhov completed the solo crossing in 159 days.

12. The longest continuous scuba dive: Ahmed Gabr

- **Details:** He spent 51 hours and 20 minutes underwater.
- **Place and Date:** Red Sea, Egypt, 2018.
- **Curiosity:** The dive was completed in deep water, with strict pressure control.

13. Fastest swim in the 200 meter butterfly: Kristóf Milák

- **Details:** World record of 1 minute, 50.73 seconds.
- **Place and Date:** Gwangju, Corea del Sud, 2019.
- **Curiosity:** Milák broke Michael Phelps' record, set in 2009.

14. The highest dive: Laso Schaller

- **Details:** He performed a dive from 58.8 meters.
- **Place and Date:** Maggia waterfall, Switzerland, 2015.
- **Curiosity:** Schaller reached a speed of 123 km/h during the dive.

15. Fastest swim in a 4x100 meter relay: United States

- **Details:** World record of 3 minutes and 8.24 seconds.
- **Place and Date:** Rio de Janeiro, Brazil, 2016.
- **Curiosity:** The team included Michael Phelps, Caleb Dressel, Ryan Held and Nathan Adrian.

16. The fastest rowing crossing of the Atlantic Ocean: The Four Oarsmen

- **Details:** They completed the crossing in 29 days and 15 hours.
- **Place and Date:** Spain-Antigua, 2017.
- **Curiosity:** The team overcame storms and adverse tides to break the record.

17. Longest swim in freezing water: Lynne Cox

- **Details:** He swam 2km in the Arctic Ocean, with water temperatures below 0°C.
- **Place and Date:** Russia, 1987.
- **Curiosity:** Cox is famous for her exploits in extreme conditions.

18. The windsurfing speed record: Antoine Albeau

- **Details:** It reached 53.27 knots (about 98.66 km/h).
- **Place and Date:** Namibia, 2015.
- **Curiosity:** Perfect wind and water conditions are crucial for this discipline.

19. The greatest depth reached while diving: Herbert Nitsch

- **Details:** He reached a depth of 253.2 meters in freediving.
- **Place and Date:** Santorini, Greece, 2012.
- **Curiosity:** Nitsch is known as "The Deepest Man in the World".

20. The record for staying on a surfboard: Mauro Cavalheiro

- **Details:** He surfed continuously for 36 hours.
- **Place and Date:** Brazil, 2021.
- **Curiosity:** The feat was completed on small waves to ensure continuity.

These records demonstrate how water, from a natural element, is transformed into an extraordinary challenge field, where athletes and enthusiasts overcome new limits every day.

6.1.3 Mountain Sports and Climbing

Mountain sports and climbing require not only physical strength, but also extraordinary mental endurance and ability to adapt. Across breathtaking peaks, rock faces and extreme routes, athletes and adventurers have set records that defy gravity and human limits. Below, 20 extraordinary records related to mountain sports and climbing.

---

1. Fastest climb of Everest: Pemba Dorje Sherpa

- **Details:** He reached the summit in 8 hours and 10 minutes.
- **Place and Date:** Monte Everest, Nepal, 2004.
- **Curiosity:** Pemba Dorje completed the climb from South Base Camp without supplementary oxygen.

---

2. Youngest person to climb Everest: Jordan Romero

- **Details:** He reached the summit at 13 years old.
- **Place and Date:** Monte Everest, Nepal, 2010.
- **Curiosity:** Romero was accompanied by an expert team, which ensured his safety.

---

3. Highest unroped climb: Alex Honnold

- **Details:** He climbed El Capitan, a 900 meter vertical wall, without ropes.
- **Place and Date:** Yosemite National Park, United States, 2017.
- **Curiosity:** This feat was chronicled in the award-winning documentary "Free Solo."

---

4. Longest stay on a rock face: Tommy Caldwell and Kevin Jorgeson

- **Details:** They spent 19 consecutive days climbing the Dawn Wall.
- **Place and Date:** Yosemite National Park, United States, 2015.
- **Curiosity:** The climb was considered one of the most difficult ever undertaken.

---

5. Fastest climb of Mount Kilimanjaro: Karl Egloff

- **Details:** He completed the climb and descent in 6 hours and 42 minutes.
- **Place and Date:** Tanzania, 2014.
- **Curiosity:** Egloff combined mountain running and endurance to set this record.

---

6. The longest mountain crossing: Reinhold Messner

- **Details:** He crossed the Andes for over 2,000 km on foot.
- **Place and Date:** Sud America, 1989.
- **Curiosity:** Messner is known for being the first to climb all 14 mountains above 8,000 meters.

---

7. Fastest climb of Monte Blanc: Kilian Jornet

- **Details:** He reached the summit in 4 hours and 57 minutes starting from Chamonix.
- **Place and Date:** France, 2013.
- **Curiosity:** Jornet is a mountain running and skyrunning legend.

---

8. The greatest feat of solo mountaineering: Hermann Buhl

- **Details:** He climbed Nanga Parbat alone.
- **Place and Date:** Pakistan, 1953.
- **Curiosity:** Buhl completed the climb without oxygen and in extreme conditions.

---

9. Highest indoor climb: Adam Ondra

- **Details:** He completed a 70 meter wall at a climbing centre.
- **Place and Date:** Czech Republic, 2021.
- **Curiosity:** Ondra is known for his technical ability and is one of the best sport climbers in the world.

---

10. Fastest climb of the Seven Summits: Colin O'Brady

- **Details:** He climbed the seven highest mountains on each continent in 132 days.
- **Place and Date:** Global, 2016.
- **Curiosity:** O'Brady completed the feat while facing extreme weather conditions.

---

11. The speed record in sport climbing: Veddriq Leonardo

- **Details:** He climbed a 15 meter wall in 5.208 seconds.
- **Place and Date:** Salt Lake City, United States, 2021.
- **Curiosity:** This discipline requires a combination of explosive strength and agility.

12. The greatest height reached in paragliding: Antoine Girard

- **Details:** He flew up to 8,157 meters above Broad Peak.
- **Place and Date:** Pakistan, 2016.
- **Curiosity:** Girard faced rarefied oxygen conditions during the flight.

13. Largest artificial climbing wall: Clymb Abu Dhabi

- **Details:** The wall measures 43 meters high.
- **Place:** Abu Dhabi, Emirati Arab Uniti.
- **Curiosity:** This center has become a tourist attraction for climbing enthusiasts.

14. The first winter climb of K2: Nepalese team

- **Details:** A team of 10 climbers reached the summit during the winter.
- **Place and Date:** Pakistan, 2021.
- **Curiosity:** This feat marked a milestone in mountaineering.

15. Longest zipline in the mountains: Jebel Jais Flight

- **Details:** It measures 2.83 km.
- **Place:** United Arab Emirates.
- **Curiosity:** The zipline passes through spectacular views in the mountains.

16. Biggest climbing competition: IFSC Climbing World Championships

- **Details:** It brings together over 500 athletes from 50 nations.

- **Place:** Various countries, every two years.
- **Curiosity:** It is the greatest event for sport climbing.

---

17. Fastest climb of the Matterhorn: Dani Arnold

- **Details:** He climbed the north face in 1 hour and 46 minutes.
- **Place and Date:** Switzerland, 2015.
- **Curiosity:** Arnold is famous for his ability to climb without ropes in record time.

---

18. Tallest slackline walk: Nathan Paulin

- **Details:** He walked on a tightrope 1,662 meters above sea level.
- **Place and Date:** Mont Blanc, France, 2019.
- **Curiosity:** The rope spanned a canyon between two peaks.

---

19. Fastest climb of Mount Aconcagua: Karl Egloff

- **Details:** He climbed and descended the mountain in 11 hours and 52 minutes.
- **Place and Date:** Argentina, 2019.
- **Curiosity:** Egloff holds speed records on several iconic mountains.

---

20. Most consecutive climbs of a wall: Alain Robert

- **Details:** He climbed the same building, the Burj Khalifa, 5 times in one day.
- **Place and Date:** Dubai, United Arab Emirates, 2020.
- **Curiosity:** Robert, known as the "French Spider-Man", often tackles urban walls without ropes.

These records demonstrate how adventure and the challenge against nature can lead humans to incredible achievements, celebrating courage and resilience.

6.2 Team Sports

Introduction

Team sports are a celebration of teamwork, strategy and collective passion. Whether it's football, basketball, rugby or other sports, each team shares a common goal: to excel and leave an indelible mark on the history of sport. In this section, we'll explore the most impressive team records, celebrating feats that demonstrate how collaboration and talent can lead to extraordinary results.

6.2.1 Team Records

Team records represent the culmination of a collective effort and a demonstration of how teamwork can overcome individual limitations. Below, 20 extraordinary records linked to the teams that wrote the history of sport.

1. The most successful team in the history of football: Real Madrid

- **Details:** He has won 14 UEFA Champions Leagues, the most ever.
- **Place and Date:** Global, since 1956.
- **Curiosity:** The team is recognized as one of the most prestigious clubs in the world.

2. The basketball team with the most NBA titles: Boston Celtics

- **Details:** He has won 17 NBA championships, tied with the Los Angeles Lakers.
- **Place and Date:** United States, since 1957.
- **Curiosity:** The Celtics dominated the league in the 1960s, winning 8 consecutive titles.

---

3. Rugby team with the most consecutive victories: All Blacks (New Zealand)

- **Details:** He recorded 18 consecutive victories in international test matches.
- **Place and Date:** Global, 2015 to 2016.
- **Curiosity:** The All Blacks are known for their traditional haka, a Maori dance performed before each match.

---

4. The winningest baseball team: New York Yankees

- **Details:** He won 27 World Series.
- **Place and Date:** United States, since 1923.
- **Curiosity:** The Yankees are one of the most recognizable and celebrated teams in professional sports.

---

5. The volleyball team with the most Olympic titles: USSR (later Russia)

- **Details:** He won 4 Olympic gold medals in men's volleyball.
- **Place and Date:** Global, since 1964.
- **Curiosity:** The team was a benchmark for Soviet dominance in sports.

---

6. The football team with the most national titles: Rangers FC

- **Details:** He won 55 Scottish Championships.
- **Place and Date:** Scotland, since 1891.

- **Curiosity:** Rangers have one of the fiercest rivalries with Celtic FC, known as the "Old Firm".

---

7. The team with the most points in an NBA season: Golden State Warriors

- **Details:** He had 73 wins in the 2015-2016 season.
- **Place and Date:** United States, 2016.
- **Curiosity:** The Warriors surpassed the Chicago Bulls' previous record.

---

8. The cricket team with the most World Cup victories: Australia

- **Details:** He has won 5 ICC World Cups.
- **Place and Date:** Global, since 1987.
- **Curiosity:** The Australians are known for their consistency and the quality of their play.

---

9. The winningest ice hockey team: Montreal Canadiens

- **Details:** He won 24 Stanley Cups.
- **Place and Date:** Canada, from 1916.
- **Curiosity:** The Canadiens are one of the founding clubs of the National Hockey League (NHL).

---

10. The American football team with the most Super Bowls won: New England Patriots

- **Details:** He won 6 Super Bowls.
- **Place and Date:** United States, since 2002.
- **Curiosity:** The team is famous for the partnership between coach Bill Belichick and quarterback Tom Brady.

---

11. The most successful Formula 1 team: Scuderia Ferrari

- **Details:** He won 16 constructors' titles.
- **Place and Date:** Global, since 1950.
- **Curiosity:** Ferrari is the only team to have participated in all seasons of the Formula 1 world championship.

12. The water polo team with the most world titles: Hungary

- **Details:** He won 9 world titles in men's water polo.
- **Place and Date:** Global, since 1973.
- **Curiosity:** Hungary is considered one of the most dominant nations in the history of water polo.

13. The football team with the most consecutive victories: Bayern Munich

- **Details:** He recorded 23 consecutive victories in UEFA competitions.
- **Place and Date:** Germany, from 2020.
- **Curiosity:** Bayern are famous for their consistency at the highest level.

14. The most successful cycling team in the Tour de France: Team Ineos (formerly Sky)

- **Details:** He won 7 editions of the Tour de France.
- **Place and Date:** France, since 2012.
- **Curiosity:** The team has dominated modern cycling thanks to strategies and scientific preparation.

15. Women's basketball team with the most Olympic titles: United States

- **Details:** He won 9 consecutive gold medals.
- **Place and Date:** Global, since 1984.
- **Curiosity:** The team is considered a dynasty in women's sports.

---

16. Rugby team with the largest margin of victory: Namibia

- **Details:** He beat Chad 142-0.
- **Place and Date:** Namibia, 2002.
- **Curiosity:** This match is one of the most lopsided victories in the history of international rugby.

---

17. Most successful women's soccer team: United States

- **Details:** He won 4 FIFA World Cups.
- **Place and Date:** Global, since 1991.
- **Curiosity:** The team has inspired generations of young female footballers around the world.

---

18. The American football team with the longest winning streak: Miami Dolphins

- **Details:** He completed a perfect season with 17 wins in 1972.
- **Place and Date:** United States, 1972.
- **Curiosity:** This perfect season remains unique in NFL history.

---

19. The team with the most titles in South American football: Boca Juniors

- **Details:** He won 6 Copa Libertadores.
- **Place and Date:** Argentina, since 1977.
- **Curiosity:** La Bombonera, Boca Juniors' stadium, is one of the most iconic in the world.

20. Most successful Davis Cup tennis team: United States

- **Details:** He won 32 Davis Cup titles.
- **Place and Date:** Global, since 1900.
- **Curiosity:** The Davis Cup is the oldest international team competition in tennis.

These records demonstrate how teamwork can reach levels of absolute excellence, becoming a source of inspiration for fans and athletes around the world.

6.2.2 Historical Matches

Historic matches represent unforgettable moments in team sport, where tension, talent and emotion combine to create legendary events. These encounters defined careers, inspired generations and set records that remain etched in the collective memory. Below, 20 extraordinary matches that marked the history of sport.

1. The most exciting football final: Italy - West Germany (4-3)

- **Details:** FIFA World Cup Semifinal.
- **Place and Date:** Mexico City, Mexico, 1970.
- **Curiosity:** Known as "The Match of the Century", the match ended in extra time with 5 goals scored.

2. The longest basketball match: Indianapolis Olympians - Rochester Royals

- **Details:** NBA game lasted 78 minutes, with 6 overtimes.
- **Place and Date:** Indianapolis, United States, 1951.

- **Curiosity:** The Olympians won 75-73 in a sports marathon.

---

3. The greatest comeback in football history: Liverpool - Milan

- **Details:** UEFA Champions League final, with Liverpool overcoming a 3-0 deficit to win on penalties.
- **Place and Date:** Istanbul, Turkey, 2005.
- **Curiosity:** The match is often referred to as "The Miracle of Istanbul".

---

4. Longest baseball game: Pawtucket Red Sox - Rochester Red Wings

- **Details:** Duration of 33 innings and 8 hours and 25 minutes.
- **Place and Date:** Pawtucket, USA, 1981.
- **Curiosity:** The match ended two months after the first postponement.

---

5. The longest tennis final: Novak Djokovic - Roger Federer

- **Details:** Lasted 4 hours and 57 minutes, with Djokovic winning 13-12 in the fifth set.
- **Place and Date:** Wimbledon, London, UK, 2019.
- **Curiosity:** It was the first final decided with a fifth set tie-break in the history of the tournament.

---

6. The most epic rugby match: New Zealand - France

- **Details:** Rugby World Cup semi-final, won 43-31 by France after a memorable comeback.
- **Place and Date:** Twickenham, UK, 1999.
- **Curiosity:** It is considered one of the greatest surprises in rugby history.

7. The most memorable basketball final: USA - USSR

- **Details:** 1972 Olympic final, won by the USSR 51-50 with a disputed refereeing decision.
- **Place and Date:** Munich, Germany, 1972.
- **Curiosity:** The United States officially protested and did not accept the silver medals.

8. The most watched football final: Argentina - Germany

- **Details:** FIFA World Cup final, won by Germany 1-0 after extra time.
- **Place and Date:** Rio de Janeiro, Brazil, 2014.
- **Curiosity:** It was followed by over a billion viewers.

9. The most memorable ice hockey match: USA - USSR

- **Details:** The "Miracle on Ice" at the 1980 Winter Olympics, won by the United States 4-3.
- **Place and Date:** Lake Placid, United States, 1980.
- **Curiosity:** The victory is considered one of the greatest sporting moments in American history.

10. The longest volleyball match: Brazil - Poland

- **Details:** Duration of 2 hours and 40 minutes, won by Poland 3-2.
- **Place and Date:** Volleyball World Cup, Tokyo, Japan, 2006.
- **Curiosity:** The match was a continuous alternation of twists and turns.

11. The most exciting American football final: Super Bowl LI

- **Details:** The New England Patriots overcame a 28-3 deficit to win 34-28 in overtime against the Atlanta Falcons.
- **Place and Date:** Houston, United States, 2017.
- **Curiosity:** It is the only Super Bowl to end in overtime.

---

12. The longest tennis match: John Isner - Nicolas Mahut

- **Details:** Lasted 11 hours and 5 minutes, with Isner winning 70-68 in the fifth set.
- **Place and Date:** Wimbledon, London, UK, 2010.
- **Curiosity:** This match lasted three consecutive days.

---

13. Longest cricket match: Test match between England and South Africa

- **Details:** Lasted 9 days, ended in a draw.
- **Place and Date:** Durban, South Africa, 1939.
- **Curiosity:** The match ended without a winner because England had to catch a train.

---

14. The biggest goal in football: AS Adema - SO Emyrne

- **Details:** The match ended 149-0, with all goals scored in protest against the referees.
- **Place and Date:** Madagascar, 2002.
- **Curiosity:** The opponent intentionally scored an own goal to challenge an referee's decision.

---

15. The most dramatic basketball final: Cleveland Cavaliers - Golden State Warriors

- **Details:** The Cavaliers rallied from a 3-1 deficit in the series to win 4-3.
- **Place and Date:** Oakland, Stati Uniti, 2016.

- **Curiosity:** LeBron James was instrumental with a historic triple double in Game 7.

---

16. The most iconic water polo match: Hungary - USSR

- **Details:** "The water battle" at the Melbourne Olympics, won 4-0 by Hungary.
- **Place and Date:** Melbourne, Australia, 1956.
- **Curiosity:** The match was played in a climate of strong political tension during the Hungarian Uprising.

---

17. The most watched rugby final: New Zealand - Australia

- **Details:** World Cup final won by the All Blacks 34-17.
- **Place and Date:** Twickenham, UK, 2015.
- **Curiosity:** The victory consolidated New Zealand's dominance in world rugby.

---

18. The biggest surprise in football: Leicester City - Premier League 2015/2016

- **Details:** Leicester won the English championship with starting odds of 5000 to 1.
- **Place and Date:** United Kingdom, 2016.
- **Curiosity:** It is considered one of the most unlikely feats in the history of sports.

---

19. Most memorable baseball game: Game 7 of the 2016 World Series

- **Details:** The Chicago Cubs defeated the Cleveland Indians 8-7 in overtime to win their first title in 108 years.
- **Place and Date:** Cleveland, United States, 2016.
- **Curiosity:** This victory put an end to the "curse of the goat".

20. Longest hockey game: Detroit Red Wings - Montreal Maroons

- **Details:** It lasted 176 minutes and 30 seconds, with the Red Wings winning 1-0.
- **Place and Date:** Montreal, Canada, 1936.
- **Curiosity:** The game was decided in the sixth overtime.

These matches not only set records, but also created memorable stories that will remain etched in global sporting culture.

6.2.3 Iconic Teams

There are teams that not only win, but become legends. Iconic teams represent more than sporting success: they embody a style of play, a philosophy and a legacy that transcends the pitch. Whether it's absolute dominance, a legendary comeback or lasting social impact, these teams have left an indelible mark on the history of sports. Below, 20 iconic teams that defined eras and disciplines.

1. Brazil 1970 (Football)

- **Details:** Winner of the 1970 FIFA World Cup, with a game considered the greatest ever.
- **Place and Date:** Mexico, 1970.
- **Curiosity:** With Pelé at his peak, this team revolutionized football with its fluid, attacking style.

2. Chicago Bulls (Basket)

- **Details:** Dominators of the NBA in the 90s, with 6 titles in 8 years.

- **Place and Date:** United States, 1991-1998.
- **Curiosity:** Led by Michael Jordan and coach Phil Jackson, they are a symbol of global sporting culture.

---

3. All Blacks 2015 (Rugby)

- **Details:** Consecutive World Cup winners, with a perfect performance.
- **Place and Date:** United Kingdom, 2015.
- **Curiosity:** Their haka and dominant play have made them one of the most respected teams.

---

4. Real Madrid (Calcio)

- **Details:** The team that won 5 consecutive European Cups from 1956 to 1960.
- **Place and Date:** Europe, 1950s.
- **Curiosity:** Real Madrid defined modern football with players like Alfredo Di Stéfano.

---

5. Dream Team (Basket)

- **Details:** United States Olympic basketball team, winner of gold in Barcelona 1992.
- **Place and Date:** Spain, 1992.
- **Curiosity:** Made up of legends such as Michael Jordan, Magic Johnson and Larry Bird, it is considered the best basketball team ever assembled.

---

6. Arsenal Invincibles (Football)

- **Details:** Unbeaten team in the Premier League in the 2003-2004 season.
- **Place and Date:** United Kingdom, 2004.

- **Curiosity:** Coached by Arsène Wenger, they set a record of 49 games without defeat.

---

7. New York Yankees (Baseball)

- **Details:** With 27 World Series titles, they are the winningest team in baseball.
- **Place and Date:** United States, since 1923.
- **Curiosity:** Baseball icons, with legends like Babe Ruth and Derek Jeter.

---

8. Australia 2003 (Cricket)

- **Details:** Winner of the World Cup without losing a single match.
- **Place and Date:** South Africa, 2003.
- **Curiosity:** The team dominated world cricket for over a decade.

---

9. AC Milan (Football)

- **Details:** Team winner of 5 European Cups between 1989 and 2007.
- **Place and Date:** Europe.
- **Curiosity:** Led by Arrigo Sacchi and Carlo Ancelotti, Milan innovated football with the "total game".

---

10. Patriots 2001-2019 (Football Americano)

- **Details:** Winners of 6 Super Bowls under the leadership of Bill Belichick and Tom Brady.
- **Place and Date:** United States.
- **Curiosity:** Their consistency of success is unprecedented in the NFL.

11. FC Barcelona (Calcio)

- **Details:** Dominators of European football under Pep Guardiola, with 14 trophies in 4 years.
- **Place and Date:** Spain, 2008-2012.
- **Curiosity:** Their tiki-taka redefined modern football.

12. Detroit Red Wings (Hockey su ghiaccio)

- **Details:** With 11 Stanley Cups, they are among the winningest teams in the NHL.
- **Place and Date:** United States, since 1936.
- **Curiosity:** Known as "The Hockeytown", they have a loyal fan base.

13. Warriors 2015-2019 (Basket)

- **Details:** 3 NBA titles in 5 years with a revolutionary game based on three-point shooting.
- **Place and Date:** United States.
- **Curiosity:** With Stephen Curry and Klay Thompson, the Warriors redefined modern basketball.

14. Brazil 1982 (Football)

- **Details:** Although they did not win the World Cup, they are remembered for their spectacular style.
- **Place and Date:** Spain, 1982.
- **Curiosity:** This team embodied the "art futebol", with stars like Zico and Sócrates.

15. Los Angeles Lakers (Basket)

- **Details:** With 17 NBA titles, they are one of the most iconic teams in sports.
- **Place and Date:** United States, since 1949.
- **Curiosity:** They had legends like Magic Johnson, Kareem Abdul-Jabbar and Kobe Bryant.

16. Ferrari (Formula 1)

- **Details:** 16 constructors' titles and 15 drivers' titles.
- **Place and Date:** Global, since 1950.
- **Curiosity:** Their dominance in the 2000s under Michael Schumacher was legendary.

17. USSR Volleyball (1960s-1980s)

- **Details:** World dominators of men's and women's volleyball.
- **Place and Date:** Global.
- **Curiosity:** Their scientific and technical approach to the game has made them unbeatable.

18. Red Sox 2004 (Baseball)

- **Details:** The team that ended the "Curse of the Bambino" by winning the World Series after 86 years.
- **Place and Date:** United States.
- **Curiosity:** The comeback against the Yankees is one of baseball's most epic stories.

19. France 1998 (Football)

- **Details:** Winners of the FIFA World Cup, hosted at home.
- **Place and Date:** France, 1998.
- **Curiosity:** Led by Zinedine Zidane, their victory was a moment of national unity.

20. Manchester United 1999 (Football)

- **Details:** Treble winners (Premier League, FA Cup, Champions League) in a single season.
- **Place and Date:** United Kingdom, 1999.
- **Curiosity:** The Champions League final against Bayern Munich is one of the most exciting ever.

These iconic teams demonstrate how talent, teamwork and determination can create legends that continue to inspire generations of athletes and fans.

6.3 Emerging Sports

Introduction

Emerging sports represent the continuous evolution of the sporting world, with new disciplines conquering an increasingly larger audience. These sports often combine technology, creativity and innovation, reflecting the cultural and social changes of our time. In this section we will explore the feats and records related to these disciplines, which are rapidly gaining prominence on the global stage.

6.3.1 eSports

ESports, or electronic sports, are video game competitions organized at a professional level. From million-dollar tournaments to global communities, eSports has transformed video games into a sporting phenomenon involving millions of players and spectators around the world. Below, 20 extraordinary records related to the world of eSports.

1. The eSports tournament with the highest prize pool: *The International 10*

- **Details:** Prize pool of 40 million dollars.
- **Place and Date:** Bucharest, Romania, 2021.
- **Curiosity:** The tournament is dedicated to *Dota 2* and the prize pool is fan-funded through the Battle Pass.

2. Highest paid eSports player: Johan "N0tail" Sundstein

- **Details:** He earned over $7.2 million.
- **Place:** Denmark.
- **Curiosity:** N0tail is a member of the two-time winning team OG *The International* consecutive.

3. Most popular eSports game: *League of Legends*

- **Details:** Over 100 million unique viewers for the 2020 World Championship.
- **Place and Date:** Global.
- **Curiosity:** The game is known for its mix of strategy and action, with a well-developed competitive scene.

4. Youngest eSports tournament winner: Victor "Lil Poison" De Leon

- **Details:** He won a tournament *Halo* at the age of 7.
- **Place and Date:** United States, 2005.
- **Curiosity:** Lil Poison is considered a video game prodigy.

5. The most used streaming platform for eSports: Twitch

- **Details:** Hosts 70% of live eSports content.
- **Place and Date:** Global, since 2011.
- **Curiosity:** Twitch has made competitive gaming accessible to millions of viewers.

---

6. Largest number of viewers for an eSports event: *Free Fire World Series*

- **Details:** 5.4 million concurrent viewers.
- **Place and Date:** Singapore, 2021.
- **Curiosity:** *Free Fire* it is particularly popular in emerging countries.

---

7. The longest eSports competition: *DreamHack* Festival

- **Details:** A 72 hour marathon of games and tournaments.
- **Place and Date:** Sweden, since 1994.
- **Curiosity:** *DreamHack* it is also a social gathering for gaming enthusiasts.

---

8. The record for kills in a single eSports game: *Hit* in *Fortnite*

- **Details:** He made 23 disposals in the World Cup final.
- **Place and Date:** United States, 2019.
- **Curiosity:** This record guaranteed him first place and 3 million dollars.

---

9. The winningest eSports team: OG

- **Details:** He won twice *The International* consecutive.
- **Place and Date:** 2018-2019.
- **Curiosity:** OG is known for its ability to innovate gaming strategies.

10. Largest live eSports event: *League of Legends World Championship 2018*

- **Details:** 99.6 million unique viewers.
- **Place and Date:** Incheon, South Korea, 2018.
- **Curiosity:** The event took place in a sold-out stadium with a memorable opening show.

---

11. Longest eSports winning streak: SK Telecom T1

- **Details:** 15 consecutive victories in championships *League of Legends*.
- **Place and Date:** South Korea, 2015.
- **Curiosity:** SK Telecom T1 is one of the most decorated teams in eSports history.

---

12. Oldest eSports player: Abbe Drakborg

- **Details:** Compete in tournaments *Counter-Strike* at the age of 78.
- **Place and Date:** Sweden, since 2018.
- **Curiosity:** It proves that gaming is a sport for all ages.

---

13. The record of earnings for an individual competition: *Hit* in *Fortnite World Cup*

- **Details:** He won $3 million in a single tournament.
- **Place and Date:** United States, 2019.
- **Curiosity:** Bugha's victory is considered one of the biggest moments in eSports.

---

14. The team with the most titles in *Counter-Strike*: Astralis

- **Details:** He won 4 Majors.
- **Place and Date:** Denmark, since 2018.
- **Curiosity:** Astralis is famous for its scientific approach to eSports.

---

15. Largest prize pool in a team event: *The International 2019*

- **Details:** OG won $15.6 million.
- **Place and Date:** Shanghai, China, 2019.
- **Curiosity:** It is the event with the highest prize pool in the history of eSports.

---

16. Record viewership for a single streamer: Ninja

- **Details:** 635,000 concurrent viewers during a session *Fortnite* con Drake.
- **Place and Date:** United States, 2018.
- **Curiosity:** This event marked a turning point in the popularity of eSports.

---

17. Most played competitive video game: *Counter-Strike: Global Offensive*

- **Details:** Over 20 million monthly active players.
- **Place and Date:** Global, since 2012.
- **Curiosity:** *CS:GO* continues to attract players and spectators for its simplicity and competitiveness.

---

18. The player with the most kills in *Call of Duty*: Expensive

- **Details:** He reached 10,000 eliminations in professional competitions.
- **Place and Date:** United States, 2020.
- **Curiosity:** Scump is a legend of the franchise *Call of Duty*.

19. The most popular eSports mobile platform: *PUBG Mobile*

- **Details:** With over 50 million daily active users.
- **Place and Date:** Global, since 2018.
- **Curiosity:** *PUBG Mobile* has made eSports accessible to millions of players in emerging countries.

---

20. The most innovative eSports league: Overwatch League

- **Details:** The first championship with teams representing cities, like in the NBA.
- **Place and Date:** Global, since 2018.
- **Curiosity:** The Overwatch League has introduced a new model for eSports structure.

ESports are no longer just a youth phenomenon, but a discipline that is redefining the concept of sporting competition. With their mix of strategy, skill and technology, they continue to grow, conquering new fans and setting incredible records.

6.3.2 Artistic Disciplines

Artistic disciplines combine creative expression with physical performance, transforming the body into a means to tell stories and arouse emotions. These emerging sports, often born from the meeting between art and movement, have won over the public thanks to their spectacularity and the talent of the athletes. In this section we will explore extraordinary records related to disciplines such as acrobatic dance, figure skating, rhythmic gymnastics and other sporting art forms.

1. Longest choreography ever performed: Guinness World Danceathon

- **Details:** A choreographed performance that lasted 35 consecutive hours.
- **Place and Date:** London, UK, 2021.
- **Curiosity:** Over 500 dancers participated, with styles ranging from ballet to hip-hop.

---

2. Highest jump in figure skating: Yuzuru Hanyu's quadruple Axel

- **Details:** Hanyu is the first skater to perform a quadruple Axel in competition.
- **Place and Date:** Japan, 2022.
- **Curiosity:** This jump is considered the most difficult in the history of skating.

---

3. The greatest number of consecutive spins: Gabriele Guerra

- **Details:** He completed 85 consecutive spins on ice.
- **Place and Date:** Milan, Italy, 2019.
- **Curiosity:** The control and balance required for this record is extraordinary.

---

4. Largest group choreography: Beijing Dance Festival

- **Details:** It involved 20,000 dancers in a synchronized choreography.
- **Place and Date:** Beijing, China, 2015.
- **Curiosity:** The performers danced to traditional Chinese music in a memorable event.

---

5. The greatest number of apparatus used in a rhythmic gymnastics routine: Alina Kabaeva

- **Details:** He performed a routine with 5 different apparatus in 2 minutes.
- **Place and Date:** Moscow, Russia, 2004.
- **Curiosity:** Kabaeva is one of the most decorated rhythmic gymnasts of all time.

---

6. The highest number of dorsal bends in a contortionism performance: Sofie Dossi

- **Details:** He performed 120 consecutive backbends.
- **Place and Date:** Los Angeles, United States, 2021.
- **Curiosity:** Sofie Dossi is famous for her unique balance and ability to combine contortionism and circus arts.

---

7. Longest aerial silk performance: Duo Phoenix

- **Details:** A performance that lasted 10 consecutive hours on aerial fabrics.
- **Place and Date:** Sydney, Australia, 2018.
- **Curiosity:** The feat required a combination of physical endurance and impeccable technique.

---

8. Most consecutive jumps on a bungee cord: Trampoline World Performers

- **Details:** They completed 500 jumps without interruption.
- **Place and Date:** Berlin, Germany, 2017.
- **Curiosity:** The group specializes in dance performances and trampoline acrobatics.

---

9. Longest hula hoop performance: Marawa Wamp

- **Details:** He rotated a hula hoop for 100 hours straight.
- **Place and Date:** London, UK, 2020.

- **Curiosity:** Marawa is a multifaceted performer who combines circus skills and showmanship.

---

10. The most Olympic medals in rhythmic gymnastics: Evgeniya Kanaeva

- **Details:** He won 2 consecutive Olympic gold medals.
- **Place and Date:** Beijing 2008, London 2012.
- **Curiosity:** Kanaeva is the only rhythmic gymnast to reach this milestone.

---

11. Highest somersault on trampoline: Ethan Swad

- **Details:** He performed a 10 meter somersault.
- **Place and Date:** New York, United States, 2022.
- **Curiosity:** Swad is an artist who combines extreme stunts and performance art.

---

12. The longest contemporary dance choreography: Dance Revolution Ensemble

- **Details:** A performance that lasted 12 hours.
- **Place and Date:** Paris, France, 2018.
- **Curiosity:** The event explored themes such as human emotion and organic movement.

---

13. The largest number of ribbons used in a rhythmic gymnastics choreography: Russian Olympic Group

- **Details:** He used 50 tapes at once.
- **Place and Date:** Rio de Janeiro, Brazil, 2016.
- **Curiosity:** The routine required perfect coordination between all the athletes.

14. Longest synchronized skating performance: Ice Unity Team

- **Details:** They skated for 6 hours straight.
- **Place and Date:** Helsinki, Finland, 2019.
- **Curiosity:** The team is famous for its precision and harmony in performances.

15. Most consecutive cartwheels performed by an individual: Samantha Lee

- **Details:** He completed 150 wheels without stopping.
- **Place and Date:** Tokyo, Japan, 2021.
- **Curiosity:** Samantha is a gymnast who combines strength, endurance and coordination.

16. Most gold medals in figure skating: Sonja Henie

- **Details:** He won 10 consecutive world titles and 3 Olympic gold medals.
- **Place and Date:** 1927-1936.
- **Curiosity:** Henie revolutionized skating with her elegance and innovative style.

17. The longest aerial hoop performance: Helena Circo

- **Details:** He performed a 5-hour consecutive performance on aerial hoop.
- **Place and Date:** Buenos Aires, Argentina, 2019.
- **Curiosity:** Helena is one of the most famous circus artists in Latin America.

18. Longest classical dance performance: Bolshoi Ballet

- **Details:** A 15-hour marathon with excerpts from the great classical ballets.
- **Place and Date:** Moscow, Russia, 2017.
- **Curiosity:** The event celebrated the company's 250th anniversary.

---

19. Most full turns on one hand: Aidan Chen

- **Details:** He performed 25 consecutive spins on one hand.
- **Place and Date:** Singapore, 2020.
- **Curiosity:** Chen is known for combining gymnastics and performance art.

---

20. The longest moving body art performance: Human Canvas Ensemble

- **Details:** An 8-hour choreography in which the painted dancers interacted with the audience.
- **Place and Date:** Sydney, Australia, 2021.
- **Curiosity:** The event combined dance, visual art and collective participation.

These records demonstrate how art and sport can merge, resulting in extraordinary performances that celebrate human talent in all its forms.

7. Curiosities and Collections

Introduction

The world of curiosities and collections is a realm where creativity and passion know no limits. Every object, no matter how small or strange, can hold a unique story and become part of an extraordinary collection. From the most unusual collections to the most eccentric feats, this section celebrates the exceptional of what is often overlooked.

7.1 Hobbies and Collecting

Introduction

Hobbies and collecting are an expression of each individual's unique personality and interests. Collecting is not just accumulating objects, but telling a story, preserving a piece of culture or satisfying a personal passion. In this section we explore incredible collections, some fascinating, others decidedly unusual, which demonstrate how varied the world of collecting can be.

7.1.1 More Unusual Items

When it comes to collecting, some enthusiasts have taken this activity to a whole new level by focusing on items that would rarely be considered "collectible." Below, 20 extraordinary collections of unusual objects that testify to the creativity and determination of their owners.

1. Largest collection of vomit bags: Niek Vermeulen

- **Details:** Over 6,290 bags from 200 airlines.
- **Place:** Netherlands.
- **Curiosity:** Each bag is cataloged with the date and flight it came from.

2. The largest collection of cocktail umbrellas: Eden Taki

- **Details:** 21,000 paper umbrellas.

- **Place:** Hawaii, United States.
- **Curiosity:** Each umbrella was collected during events or trips.

---

3. The largest collection of shark teeth: Vito Bertucci

- **Details:** More than 25,000 teeth, including Megalodon fossils.
- **Place:** United States.
- **Curiosity:** Bertucci found many of these fossils during sea dives.

---

4. Largest collection of corkscrews: Donald Bull

- **Details:** Over 30,000 corkscrews.
- **Place:** California, United States.
- **Curiosity:** The collection includes corkscrews that date back to the 17th century.

---

5. Largest collection of unopened chocolate bars: Bob McMillan

- **Details:** 1,500 tablets from all over the world.
- **Place:** United Kingdom.
- **Curiosity:** Each tablet is stored in a controlled environment to prevent it from deteriorating.

---

6. Largest collection of glass eyes: Dr. Henry Fechner

- **Details:** 500 glass eyes.
- **Place:** Germany.
- **Curiosity:** The collection includes ancient pieces used as medical prosthetics.

---

7. Largest collection of roller skates: Michael Sanderson

- **Details:** 2,100 pairs of skates.
- **Place:** United States.
- **Curiosity:** The collection ranges from vintage models to those used in professional competitions.

8. Largest collection of ventriloquist puppets: Terry Bennett

- **Details:** 570 puppets.
- **Place:** United States.
- **Curiosity:** Some of the puppets date back to the 1930s and are rare pieces.

9. Greatest Soap Collection: Carol Vaughan

- **Details:** 5,000 bars of soap of different shapes and fragrances.
- **Place:** Australia.
- **Curiosity:** Many bars of soap are souvenirs from hotels around the world.

10. Largest collection of lapel pins: Leon Glickman

- **Details:** Oltre 80,000 play.
- **Place:** United States.
- **Curiosity:** The collection includes pins commemorating historical events.

11. Largest perfume bottle collection: Elizabeth Bower

- **Details:** 15,000 bottles of perfume.
- **Place:** France.

- **Curiosity:** The collection includes ancient and modern bottles, many of which are unique pieces.

---

12. Largest pencil collection: Emilio Arenas

- **Details:** 24,000 pencils of different brands and designs.
- **Place:** Uruguay.
- **Curiosity:** Arenas began his collection in the 1950s and continues to enrich it.

---

13. Strangest stamp collection: Aksel Johansen

- **Details:** Stamps depicting unusual animals such as insects and reptiles.
- **Place:** Norway.
- **Curiosity:** The collection is thematic, with stamps from over 50 countries.

---

14. Largest collection of puppets: Luigi Rossi

- **Details:** 700 puppets from different cultures.
- **Place:** Italy.
- **Curiosity:** Each puppet represents a unique theatrical tradition.

---

15. Largest collection of colored vinyl: Chris Goel

- **Details:** 10,000 vinyl records of unique colors and designs.
- **Place:** United Kingdom.
- **Curiosity:** Vinyls include limited editions and promotional records.

---

16. Largest sardine can collection: Jacques Leclerc

- **Details:** 2,500 cans of sardines, many still sealed.
- **Place:** France.
- **Curiosity:** Each tin represents a different brand or limited edition.

---

17. Largest collection of Coca-Cola bottles: Gary Acheson

- **Details:** 5,000 unique bottles.
- **Place:** United States.
- **Curiosity:** Includes commemorative and rare bottles from around the world.

---

18. The largest collection of decorative plates: Maria Lopez

- **Details:** 12,000 dishes from different countries.
- **Place:** Spain.
- **Curiosity:** Each dish is a piece of local or artisanal history.

---

19. Largest collection of bottle caps: Hans Mayer

- **Details:** 20,000 bottle caps.
- **Place:** Germany.
- **Curiosity:** The collection includes historical caps of now disappeared beers.

---

20. Largest collection of lighters: Ricardo Garcia

- **Details:** 35,000 lighters of different brands and designs.
- **Place:** Mexico.
- **Curiosity:** Includes vintage lighters and unique custom-made pieces.

These examples of unusual collections demonstrate how collecting can be a form of personal expression, capable of transforming everyday objects into unique treasures.

7.1.2 Games Records

Games, both traditional and modern, are fertile ground for extraordinary feats. From board games to video games, through card and board games, each competition represents a challenge of skill, strategy and creativity. In this section we will explore 20 incredible records achieved in different types of games.

1. The longest chess match: Ivan Nikolic vs. Goran Arsovic

- **Details:** The game lasted 20 hours and 15 minutes, with 269 moves.
- **Place and Date:** Belgrade, Yugoslavia, 1989.
- **Curiosity:** The match ended in a draw, demonstrating the players' mental toughness.

2. Most simultaneous chess games: Ehsan Ghaem-Maghami

- **Details:** He played 604 matches at one time.
- **Place and Date:** Tehran, Iran, 2011.
- **Curiosity:** He won 97% of his matches, setting a new standard for simultaneous play.

3. The largest Jenga tower ever built: Kelvin Parker

- **Details:** The tower reached a height of 5.07 meters.
- **Place and Date:** Chicago, United States, 2018.

- **Curiosity:** The tower was built with 485 blocks without collapsing.

---

4. Longest Monopoly Game: Students at the University of Pittsburgh

- **Details:** The match lasted 70 consecutive days.
- **Place and Date:** Pittsburgh, United States, 1975.
- **Curiosity:** The players took turns to respect the rules of the game.

---

5. Most Rubik's Cubes solved in one hour: Feliks Zemdegs

- **Details:** He solved 301 cubes in 60 minutes.
- **Place and Date:** Melbourne, Australia, 2020.
- **Curiosity:** Zemdegs is a speedcubing champion known for his incredible speed.

---

6. The largest Pokémon card tournament: Pokémon World Championships

- **Details:** Over 7,000 participants from all over the world.
- **Place and Date:** Washington D.C., United States, 2019.
- **Curiosity:** The event included players of all ages and skill levels.

---

7. The longest card game: Bridge game

- **Details:** It lasted 145 consecutive hours.
- **Place and Date:** Springfield, United States, 1974.
- **Curiosity:** The players took turns with minimal breaks to set the record.

---

8. Highest score ever recorded in Tetris: Jonas Neubauer

- **Details:** He reached 1,248,000 points in classic mode.
- **Place and Date:** Portland, United States, 2018.
- **Curiosity:** Neubauer was a legend in the Tetris community until his passing.

9. Most dice rolled and left stacked: Zakir Hussain

- **Details:** He stacked 22 dice after a single roll.
- **Place and Date:** New Delhi, India, 2021.
- **Curiosity:** The undertaking required absolute precision and manual dexterity.

10. Risk's Greatest Game: Players United Convention

- **Details:** 1,000 participants in a single match.
- **Place and Date:** Berlin, Germany, 2015.
- **Curiosity:** The match lasted 3 days and was a celebratory event for fans of the game.

11. Longest ping pong match: Daniel Ives and Peter Ives

- **Details:** The match lasted 101 hours.
- **Place and Date:** Bristol, UK, 2020.
- **Curiosity:** The two brothers set the record for raising money for charity.

12. Most runs scored in a bowling game: Tommy Cacioppo

- **Details:** He scored 900 runs (12 consecutive strikes).
- **Place and Date:** New York, United States, 2012.
- **Curiosity:** This perfect score is very rare in competitive bowling.

13. Most players in an online chess tournament: Chess.com Championship

- **Details:** Over 30,000 participants.
- **Place and Date:** Global, 2021.
- **Curiosity:** The tournament demonstrated the growing popularity of digital chess.

14. The largest human domino: World Domino Association

- **Details:** 10,000 people arranged in a domino sequence.
- **Place and Date:** Beijing, China, 2018.
- **Curiosity:** Human dominoes required months of planning and coordination.

15. Longest video game session: Okan Kaya

- **Details:** He played *Call of Duty* per 135 ore consecutive.
- **Place and Date:** Sydney, Australia, 2012.
- **Curiosity:** He observed strict breaks to ensure his health during the attempt.

16. The largest number of Lego bricks used in a single construction: Landmarks Project

- **Details:** 5 million pieces to create a model of Big Ben.
- **Place and Date:** London, UK, 2016.
- **Curiosity:** The construction was exhibited as a temporary installation.

17. Biggest board game tournament: Essen Spiel Convention

- **Details:** Over 50,000 participants.
- **Place and Date:** Essen, Germany, every year.
- **Curiosity:** It is the largest fair in the world dedicated to board games.

---

18. The longest UNO card game: Uno World Marathon

- **Details:** It lasted 28 hours.
- **Place and Date:** Chicago, United States, 2019.
- **Curiosity:** The players competed without significant breaks to set the record.

---

19. Most puzzles completed in 24 hours: Chen Qi

- **Details:** 50 puzzles completed in one day.
- **Place and Date:** Beijing, China, 2020.
- **Curiosity:** The puzzles had varying difficulty levels, some with more than 2,000 pieces.

---

20. Largest collection of board games: Scott Snider

- **Details:** Over 3,000 games.
- **Place:** United States.
- **Curiosity:** The collection includes vintage pieces, rare games and limited editions.

These records demonstrate that every game, regardless of its nature, offers opportunities for extraordinary feats and unforgettable moments.

7.2 Food and Drinks

Introduction

The world of food and drink is not only a pleasure for the palate, but also a fertile ground for extraordinary records. From the largest dishes ever prepared to the most incredible culinary challenges, this section celebrates the creativity, mastery and ambition of cooks, chefs and enthusiasts from around the world. We will explore culinary ventures that have left their mark, proving that a passion for food can transcend all limits.

7.2.1 Larger Plates

Preparing gigantic dishes is a challenge that requires organization, skill and often an entire community of people. These dishes are not only records of greatness, but also symbols of celebration and sharing. Below, 20 extraordinary dishes that have set world records for their size.

1. The largest pizza in the world

- **Details:** A pizza measuring 1,261.65 square meters.
- **Place and Date:** Los Angeles, United States, 2023.
- **Curiosity:** The pizza was prepared with over 6,000 kg of dough, 2,000 kg of cheese and 1,500 kg of tomato sauce.

2. The longest sandwich ever made

- **Details:** A 735 meter sandwich.
- **Place and Date:** Beirut, Lebanon, 2011.
- **Curiosity:** The sandwich was prepared by over 300 volunteers and contained tuna, salad and sauces.

3. The largest cake in the world

- **Details:** A 6,500 kg cake.
- **Place and Date:** Alcobendas, Spain, 2018.
- **Curiosity:** The chocolate and vanilla themed cake was served to more than 10,000 people.

4. The largest bowl of pasta

- **Details:** 7,900 kg of spaghetti.
- **Place and Date:** Garden Grove, United States, 2010.
- **Curiosity:** The giant bowl was prepared for a community celebration.

5. The longest kebab in the world

- **Details:** A kebab at 2,000 feet.
- **Place and Date:** Ankara, Türkiye, 2018.
- **Curiosity:** The preparation required 5,000 kg of meat and hundreds of skewers.

6. The largest ice cream ever made

- **Details:** A 3 meter tall ice cream cone.
- **Place and Date:** Norway, 2015.
- **Curiosity:** The giant cone contained 1,080 liters of vanilla ice cream.

7. The biggest fruit salad

- **Details:** 20,100 kg of fruit.
- **Place and Date:** Chennai, India, 2016.
- **Curiosity:** The preparation required over 100 types of fruit and a huge team of volunteers.

8. The largest omelette ever cooked

- **Details:** A 6,466 kg omelette.
- **Place and Date:** Santarém, Portogallo, 2012.
- **Curiosity:** Over 145,000 eggs were used to prepare this record.

---

9. The biggest bowl of ramen

- **Details:** A 4,000 liter bowl of ramen.
- **Place and Date:** Tokyo, Japan, 2019.
- **Curiosity:** The giant ramen was served in a custom bowl built especially for the event.

---

10. The biggest cheesecake

- **Details:** A 4,240 kg cake.
- **Place and Date:** New York, United States, 2017.
- **Curiosity:** The cake was made for a special celebration of National Cheesecake Day.

---

11. The biggest hamburger bun

- **Details:** A 1,164 kg hamburger.
- **Place and Date:** Minnesota, USA, 2012.
- **Curiosity:** The burger was topped with 20kg of lettuce, 25kg of onions and 10kg of pickles.

---

12. The largest soup in the world

- **Details:** A soup of 26,658 litres.
- **Place and Date:** Poços de Caldas, Brazil, 2021.
- **Curiosity:** The soup was distributed free of charge to participants of a food festival.

13. The largest paella pan

- **Details:** A paella weighing 22,500 kg.
- **Place and Date:** Valencia, Spain, 2001.
- **Curiosity:** The paella was prepared in a custom-built giant pan.

14. The longest dessert: Tiramisu

- **Details:** A 266 meter tiramisu.
- **Place and Date:** Milan, Italy, 2015.
- **Curiosity:** The dessert was prepared with over 100,000 ladyfingers and 5,000 liters of mascarpone.

15. The largest chocolate sculpture

- **Details:** A 10,000 kg chocolate sculpture in the shape of a train.
- **Place and Date:** Brussels, Belgium, 2012.
- **Curiosity:** The sculpture was created to celebrate the Belgian chocolate tradition.

16. The biggest pancake ever made

- **Details:** A pancake 15 meters in diameter.
- **Place and Date:** Rochdale, UK, 1994.
- **Curiosity:** The giant pancake was shot using special equipment.

17. The longest sushi ever made

- **Details:** A 2,500 meter sushi roll.

222

- **Place and Date:** Yekaterinburg, Russia, 2017.
- **Curiosity:** The sushi was stuffed with cucumber, rice and salmon.

---

18. The greatest cocktail ever served

- **Details:** 32,000 liters of Margarita cocktails.
- **Place and Date:** Las Vegas, United States, 2012.
- **Curiosity:** The drink was served in a specially constructed giant glass.

---

19. The tallest wedding cake

- **Details:** A cake 7.8 meters high.
- **Place and Date:** Connecticut, United States, 2004.
- **Curiosity:** The cake had 7 tiers and served over 15,000 people.

---

20. The largest butter sculpture

- **Details:** A 1,200 kg sculpture depicting a cow.
- **Place and Date:** Ohio, United States, 2019.
- **Curiosity:** The sculpture was displayed at an agricultural fair to celebrate the dairy industry.

Not only are these plates extraordinarily large, they also represent the dedication, creativity and love of food of those who made them. Each record is a celebration of the human ability to transform food into something unique and memorable.

7.2.2 Gastronomic Competitions

Food competitions celebrate culinary talent, endurance and passion for food. Whether it's challenges for the most foods consumed or skill in preparing complex dishes, these competitions attract participants and spectators from all over the world. Below, 20 extraordinary records achieved in gastronomic competitions.

---

1. Most hot dogs eaten in 10 minutes: Joey Chestnut

- **Details:** 76 hot dog.
- **Place and Date:** Nathan's Famous Hot Dog Eating Contest, New York, Stati Uniti, 2021.
- **Curiosity:** Chestnut is a legend of competitive eating, with numerous titles to his name.

---

2. The greatest pizza eating competition: Michele Galli

- **Details:** 10 margherita pizzas in 15 minutes.
- **Place and Date:** Naples, Italy, 2018.
- **Curiosity:** The competition celebrated the tradition of Neapolitan pizza.

---

3. The most crowded pie eating contest

- **Details:** 500 participants ate cakes at the same time.
- **Place and Date:** London, UK, 2017.
- **Curiosity:** The event was organized to raise funds for charity.

---

4. Most chicken wings eaten in 30 minutes: Molly Schuyler

- **Details:** 501 chicken wings.
- **Place and Date:** Philadelphia Wing Bowl, United States, 2018.
- **Curiosity:** Schuyler is one of the most famous competitive eaters in the world.

5. The hottest chili competition ever held

- **Details:** Participants ate Carolina Reaper chili peppers, the hottest in the world.
- **Place and Date:** Carolina Reaper Challenge, United States, 2019.
- **Curiosity:** The competition was won by a contestant who ate 20 chili peppers.

6. Most cupcakes eaten in 5 minutes

- **Details:** 72 cupcake.
- **Place and Date:** Los Angeles, United States, 2016.
- **Curiosity:** The winner used a quick technique to reduce chewing time.

7. The longest non-stop cooking competition

- **Details:** 72 ore consecutive.
- **Place and Date:** Kerala, India, 2017.
- **Curiosity:** Participants prepared over 1,000 traditional dishes during the event.

8. Most burgers eaten in 3 minutes

- **Details:** 12 hamburger.
- **Place and Date:** Tokyo, Japan, 2019.
- **Curiosity:** The winner broke the previous record by 10 burgers.

9. The biggest milk drinking contest

- **Details:** 1 liter of milk in 10 seconds.
- **Place and Date:** Wisconsin, United States, 2015.
- **Curiosity:** The competition attracted dairy enthusiasts.

---

10. The longest running barbecue competition

- **Details:** 48 consecutive hours of cooking.
- **Place and Date:** Texas, United States, 2018.
- **Curiosity:** The event included teams preparing ribs, brisket and chicken.

---

11. The fastest sushi making competition

- **Details:** 100 pieces of sushi eaten in 3 minutes.
- **Place and Date:** Osaka, Japan, 2021.
- **Curiosity:** The winner demonstrated impeccable technique in using the chopsticks.

---

12. The world's largest beer competition

- **Details:** 1,000 participants.
- **Place and Date:** Oktoberfest, Monaco, Germania, 2019.
- **Curiosity:** The event saw attendees drinking beer from 1-litre steins.

---

13. The most competitive lobster roll eating contest

- **Details:** 30 sandwiches eaten in 10 minutes.
- **Place and Date:** Maine Lobster Festival, United States, 2022.
- **Curiosity:** The competition celebrates Maine's famous lobster roll.

---

14. The fastest ice cream eating race

- **Details:** 5 liters of ice cream eaten in 10 minutes.
- **Place and Date:** Rome, Italy, 2020.
- **Curiosity:** The competition included several variations of artisanal ice cream.

15. The longest donut eating contest

- **Details:** 500 donuts consumed in one hour by a group of 10 participants.
- **Place and Date:** New York, United States, 2018.
- **Curiosity:** Each participant received a certificate of participation.

16. The largest pasta making competition in the world

- **Details:** 300 participants ate spaghetti with tomato sauce.
- **Place and Date:** Bologna, Italy, 2016.
- **Curiosity:** The event celebrated the tradition of Italian cuisine.

17. The most competitive taco eating contest

- **Details:** 126 tacos eaten in 8 minutes.
- **Place and Date:** Tijuana, Mexico, 2019.
- **Curiosity:** The winner surpassed the previous record of 103 tacos.

18. The Biggest Hot Pot Competition

- **Details:** 500 people ate hot pot together.
- **Place and Date:** Chengdu, China, 2021.

- **Curiosity:** The event included traditional flavors and local ingredients.

---

19. The most slices of cake eaten in 1 minute

- **Details:** 15 slices.
- **Place and Date:** London, UK, 2018.
- **Curiosity:** The winner used only his hands, as required by the rules.

---

20. The biggest coffee drinking competition

- **Details:** 1,000 cups of espresso consumed by 100 participants.
- **Place and Date:** Milan, Italy, 2017.
- **Curiosity:** The event celebrated the culture of Italian coffee.

These culinary records demonstrate that food is not just nourishment, but also a source of challenge, entertainment, and cultural celebration. Each competition represents a unique mix of skill, endurance and passion for gastronomy.

8. Youth and Kids' Zone

Introduction

The Youth and Kids' Zone section celebrates the extraordinary feats of the youngest. Records set by children and teenagers prove that talent, passion and determination are ageless. From sports fields to artistic performances, from technical skills to innovative ideas, this section collects the stories of kids who have achieved incredible goals, inspiring peers and adults around the world.

8.1 Record Under 16

Introduction

The under 16 records highlight how youngsters can excel in a variety of disciplines. These achievements not only highlight extraordinary abilities, but also testify to the limitless potential that lies in the younger generation. In this section, we will explore sporting, artistic and creative feats carried out by young talents, capable of surprising and inspiring.

8.1.1 Sports Talents

Sport is one of the areas in which young people often demonstrate extraordinary skills, achieving results that rival those of adults. Below, 20 sporting records set by children under 16, which highlight the energy, dedication and talent of the new generations.

1. The youngest professional footballer: Mauricio Baldivieso

- **Details:** He made his debut at the age of 12 in a first division match.
- **Place and Date:** Bolivia, 2009.
- **Curiosity:** His father was the coach of the team, but Mauricio proved he deserved his place on the pitch.

2. The youngest winner of a tennis tournament: Martina Hingis

- **Details:** He won a professional tournament at 14 years old.
- **Place and Date:** Hamburg, Germany, 1994.
- **Curiosity:** Hingis has become one of the most famous tennis players in the world.

3. The youngest Formula 4 champion: Andrea Kimi Antonelli

- **Details:** He won the championship at 15 years old.
- **Place and Date:** Italy, 2021.
- **Curiosity:** Antonelli is considered one of the promises of international motorsport.

4. Youngest marathon runner: Budhia Singh

- **Details:** He ran a marathon at 5 years old.
- **Place and Date:** India, 2006.
- **Curiosity:** His feat has raised discussions about child safety in extreme sports.

5. Youngest Everest climber: Jordan Romero

- **Details:** He reached the summit at 13 years old.
- **Place and Date:** Nepal, 2010.
- **Curiosity:** Jordan was accompanied by an experienced team and his father.

6. The youngest skateboarding champion: Sky Brown

- **Details:** He won a professional title at 10 years old.
- **Place and Date:** United States, 2018.
- **Curiosity:** Sky is also a surfer and an inspiration to young athletes.

7. Youngest Olympic Swimmer: Marjorie Gestring

- **Details:** He won a gold medal in diving at 13.
- **Place and Date:** Berlin, Germany, 1936.

- **Curiosity:** She is still the youngest Olympic gold medalist in history.

---

8. Youngest winner of a horse riding competition: Jessica Mendoza

- **Details:** He won a Grand Prix at 14.
- **Place and Date:** United Kingdom, 2010.
- **Curiosity:** Jessica has become a point of reference in youth riding.

---

9. The youngest sport climbing champion: Ashima Shiraishi

- **Details:** He climbed a 9a difficulty route at the age of 13.
- **Place and Date:** Japan, 2014.
- **Curiosity:** Ashima is considered a climbing prodigy.

---

10. Youngest winner of a track cycling race: Thomas Pidcock

- **Details:** He won a national competition at 15 years old.
- **Place and Date:** United Kingdom, 2014.
- **Curiosity:** Pidcock is now one of the best professional cyclists in the world.

---

11. The youngest champion figure skater: Tara Lipinski

- **Details:** He won the World Championships at 14.
- **Place and Date:** Lausanne, Switzerland, 1997.
- **Curiosity:** Lipinski revolutionized figure skating with his innovative technique.

---

12. Youngest surfing champion: Kelly Slater

- **Details:** He won his first national title at 12 years old.
- **Place and Date:** Florida, United States, 1984.
- **Curiosity:** Slater became a surfing legend with 11 world titles.

---

13. Youngest road race winner: Max Woosey

- **Details:** He completed a 10km run at age 7.
- **Place and Date:** United Kingdom, 2015.
- **Curiosity:** Max continued to participate in charity events.

---

14. The youngest Olympic gymnast: Nadia Comaneci

- **Details:** He won 3 gold medals at 14 years old.
- **Place and Date:** Montreal, Canada, 1976.
- **Curiosity:** Comaneci was the first gymnast to achieve a perfect score of 10.

---

15. Youngest golf champion: Michelle Wie

- **Details:** He won a professional tournament at 13 years old.
- **Place and Date:** Hawaii, United States, 2003.
- **Curiosity:** Michelle has become one of the most influential golfers of her generation.

---

16. The youngest athletics champion: Armand Duplantis

- **Details:** He set a youth world record in the pole vault at 15.
- **Place and Date:** Sweden, 2015.
- **Curiosity:** Duplantis is now one of the best athletes in the world in his discipline.

---

17. Youngest professional alpine skier: Mikaela Shiffrin

- **Details:** He won a World Cup race at 16.
- **Place and Date:** Sweden, 2011.
- **Curiosity:** Shiffrin has become an alpine skiing legend.

---

18. Youngest mixed martial arts athlete: Victoria Lee

- **Details:** He won a professional fight at 16.
- **Place and Date:** Singapore, 2021.
- **Curiosity:** Lee is considered a promising player in MMA.

---

19. The youngest archery champion: Deepika Kumari

- **Details:** He won the World Youth Championship at 14.
- **Place and Date:** Türkiye, 2009.
- **Curiosity:** Deepika has become a symbol for archery in India.

---

20. Youngest marathon winner: Budhia Singh

- **Details:** He completed a marathon at 4 years old.
- **Place and Date:** India, 2005.
- **Curiosity:** His story has inspired documentaries and discussions on the ethics of children's sports.

These young athletes demonstrate that with commitment and determination it is possible to achieve extraordinary goals, even at an early age. Their exploits represent the essence of the sporting spirit and inspire future generations.

8.1.2 Artistic Records

Art is a form of expression that transcends age, and young talents often amaze with their creativity, technique and capacity for innovation. The artistic records set by children and adolescents demonstrate that a passion for art can lead to extraordinary results, inspiring other young people to cultivate their dreams. Below, 20 extraordinary artistic records achieved by under 16s.

---

1. Youngest painter to exhibit in a gallery: Aelita Andre

- **Details:** He exhibited his first collection at just 2 years old.
- **Place and Date:** Melbourne, Australia, 2010.
- **Curiosity:** Aelita's works, often abstract, have been described as surprising and innovative.

---

2. Youngest musician to release an album: Ethan Bortnick

- **Details:** He released his first piano album at 6 years old.
- **Place and Date:** Florida, United States, 2007.
- **Curiosity:** Ethan is also a prodigy pianist, capable of playing complex compositions from memory.

---

3. Youngest ballet dancer to perform professionally: Julian Mackay

- **Details:** He made his debut with the Royal Ballet at 12.
- **Place and Date:** London, UK, 2010.
- **Curiosity:** Mackay is considered one of the brightest promises of contemporary ballet.

---

4. The youngest conductor: José Angel Salazar

- **Details:** He conducted a symphony orchestra at 8 years old.
- **Place and Date:** Caracas, Venezuela, 2012.

- **Curiosity:** Salazar impressed audiences with his technical mastery and charisma.

---

5. The youngest sculptor exhibited in a museum: Arushi Bhatnagar

- **Details:** He presented a sculpture at 11 years old.
- **Place and Date:** New Delhi, India, 2018.
- **Curiosity:** His work represented a message of environmental awareness.

---

6. Youngest published book illustrator: Dami Lee

- **Details:** He illustrated a children's book at 9 years old.
- **Place and Date:** South Korea, 2015.
- **Curiosity:** The book became a bestseller in his country.

---

7. Youngest photography contest winner: Zev Hoover

- **Details:** He won an international competition at 14 years old.
- **Place and Date:** United States, 2014.
- **Curiosity:** His photographs used creative techniques to create surreal worlds.

---

8. The youngest actor to win a film award: Quvenzhané Wallis

- **Details:** He won an award at age 9 for the film *King of the Savage Land.*
- **Place and Date:** United States, 2012.
- **Curiosity:** She was also nominated for an Oscar, the youngest actress in the history of the Academy.

---

9. Youngest violinist to perform at Carnegie Hall: Sarah Chang

- **Details:** He played in concert at 8 years old.
- **Place and Date:** New York, United States, 1989.
- **Curiosity:** Chang has become one of the most acclaimed violinists in the world.

---

10. Youngest published novelist: Dorothy Straight

- **Details:** He published his first book at 6 years old.
- **Place and Date:** United States, 1964.
- **Curiosity:** The novel, written for his grandmother, was praised for its sincerity and imagination.

---

11. Youngest Choreographer: Akshat Singh

- **Details:** He created a choreography for a group of dancers at 8 years old.
- **Place and Date:** Mumbai, India, 2016.
- **Curiosity:** Singh is also known for his spectacular performances in talent shows.

---

12. Youngest artist to create a public mural: Keiron Williamson

- **Details:** He completed a mural at 10 years old.
- **Place and Date:** Norwich, UK, 2015.
- **Curiosity:** Williamson is known as the "mini Monet" for his early talent in painting.

---

13. Youngest design competition winner: Emily Brooke

- **Details:** He won an industrial design competition at 14.
- **Place and Date:** San Francisco, United States, 2019.

- **Curiosity:** His project was an eco-friendly lamp made from recycled materials.

---

14. Youngest pianist to play with a symphony orchestra: Maxim Lando

- **Details:** He played with the Moscow Philharmonic at 11.
- **Place and Date:** Moscow, Russia, 2015.
- **Curiosity:** Lando has been called a rare talent by music critics.

---

15. Youngest singer to win a talent show: Jackie Evancho

- **Details:** He won a musical talent show at 10 years old.
- **Place and Date:** United States, 2010.
- **Curiosity:** Jackie became an international star for her extraordinary opera voice.

---

16. Youngest graffiti artist: Kieron Williamson

- **Details:** He completed his first mural at 9 years old.
- **Place and Date:** London, UK, 2017.
- **Curiosity:** Williamson combined urban art and ecological themes in his graffiti.

---

17. Youngest Theater Acting Award Winner: Aiden Marshall

- **Details:** He won an award for best theater performance at 13.
- **Place and Date:** New York, United States, 2021.
- **Curiosity:** His performance was praised for its emotion and intensity.

---

18. The youngest participant in an opera performance: Alma Deutscher

- **Details:** He made his debut in an opera at 7 years old.
- **Place and Date:** Vienna, Austria, 2012.
- **Curiosity:** Alma is also a talented composer.

---

19. The youngest digital artist: Carlito Rios

- **Details:** He created a series of digital works at 8 years old.
- **Place and Date:** Los Angeles, United States, 2020.
- **Curiosity:** His works have been sold as NFTs to collectors around the world.

---

20. The youngest fashion designer: Cecilia Cassini

- **Details:** He presented his first collection at 10 years old.
- **Place and Date:** California, United States, 2015.
- **Curiosity:** Cecilia has been called a fashion prodigy, with a unique eye for design.

These young artists demonstrate that age is no limit to creativity. Their endeavors celebrate the talent and passion that emerges from an early age, inspiring future generations.

8.2 Challenges for the younger ones

Introduction

Youth Challenges represent an opportunity for children and adolescents to test themselves in unique and stimulating ways. These records not only demonstrate the determination and creativity of the participants, but also promote fun and sharing experiences among peers. Challenges range from physical activities and games to creative and technical feats, making this section a tribute to the vitality and energy of the new generations.

20 Extraordinary Challenges for the Youngest

1. The tallest human pyramid made by children

- **Details:** 25 children created a 5 meter high pyramid.
- **Place and Date:** Barcelona, Spain, 2019.
- **Curiosity:** The challenge required weeks of training to ensure stability and safety.

2. The most jump ropes in one minute

- **Details:** 230 jumps performed by a 10 year old boy.
- **Place and Date:** Tokyo, Japan, 2021.
- **Curiosity:** The challenge was performed without errors, showing agility and endurance.

3. The tallest Lego tower built by a team of children

- **Details:** A 12 meter tower built in 5 hours.
- **Place and Date:** London, UK, 2018.
- **Curiosity:** The children used over 50,000 Lego bricks.

4. The highest number of balloons inflated in one hour

- **Details:** A group of children inflated 1,000 balloons.
- **Place and Date:** Sydney, Australia, 2020.
- **Curiosity:** The challenge was part of a fundraiser for charity.

5. The largest puzzle completed by children

- **Details:** A 24,000 piece puzzle completed in 3 days.
- **Place and Date:** New York, United States, 2022.
- **Curiosity:** The challenge involved 50 children, demonstrating teamwork and patience.

6. The largest number of books read by a class in a month

- **Details:** A class of 30 students read 500 books.
- **Place and Date:** Toronto, Canada, 2019.
- **Curiosity:** Each student contributed by reading at least 10 books.

7. The longest chain of dominoes built by children

- **Details:** A chain of 25,000 pieces.
- **Place and Date:** Berlin, Germany, 2018.
- **Curiosity:** The sequence was completed in 7 minutes without interruption.

8. The largest number of soap bubbles blown at once

- **Details:** 300 children blew bubbles at the same time.
- **Place and Date:** Mumbai, India, 2021.
- **Curiosity:** The challenge created a colorful and fun show.

9. The longest running relay organized by children

- **Details:** A relay race that lasted 12 hours with 200 children.
- **Place and Date:** Johannesburg, South Africa, 2020.

- **Curiosity:** Each participant ran 500 meters, maintaining the pace throughout.

---

10. Most sand castles built in one hour

- **Details:** 1,200 castles made by 150 children.
- **Place and Date:** Miami, United States, 2019.
- **Curiosity:** Each castle had to meet height and stability criteria.

---

11. The biggest kite flying competition

- **Details:** 500 children flew their kites at the same time.
- **Place and Date:** Beijing, China, 2018.
- **Curiosity:** Each kite was uniquely decorated by the participants.

---

12. The most soccer balls kicked in one minute

- **Details:** 120 balls kicked into a net by a team of children.
- **Place and Date:** Madrid, Spain, 2021.
- **Curiosity:** Each child had a maximum time of 10 seconds to score.

---

13. The biggest painting competition

- **Details:** 1,000 children painted simultaneously on a giant canvas.
- **Place and Date:** Paris, France, 2020.
- **Curiosity:** The final painting represented a mosaic of personal colors and themes.

---

14. The most party hats worn simultaneously

- **Details:** 600 children wore colorful hats.
- **Place and Date:** Rio de Janeiro, Brazil, 2019.
- **Curiosity:** The challenge was part of an event to celebrate Carnival.

---

15. The longest obstacle course completed by children

- **Details:** A 3km course with 15 obstacles.
- **Place and Date:** Melbourne, Australia, 2022.
- **Curiosity:** Each obstacle was designed to test balance, strength and speed.

---

16. Most snowballs thrown in one minute

- **Details:** 500 snowballs thrown by 50 children.
- **Place and Date:** Helsinki, Finland, 2021.
- **Curiosity:** The challenge took place in a snow-covered park during the winter.

---

17. The most paper bows cut in 10 minutes

- **Details:** 2,000 bows created by a group of 100 children.
- **Place and Date:** Oslo, Norway, 2019.
- **Curiosity:** The challenge required precision and speed in creating the bows.

---

18. The largest tower of stacked glasses

- **Details:** A 10 meter high tower built with plastic cups.
- **Place and Date:** Chicago, United States, 2020.
- **Curiosity:** The children worked as a team to build the tower without causing it to collapse.

19. Most origami folded in one hour

- **Details:** 3,000 origami pieces created by 200 children.
- **Place and Date:** Kyoto, Japan, 2018.
- **Curiosity:** Each participant folded at least 15 animal-themed origami.

20. The largest mosaic created with bottle caps

- **Details:** A 30 square meter mosaic created with 50,000 corks.
- **Place and Date:** Nairobi, Kenya, 2021.
- **Curiosity:** The work represented a message of awareness on ecology.

These challenges demonstrate that even the youngest can achieve extraordinary goals, turning fun and collaboration into unforgettable records.

9. Travel and Explorations

Introduction

Traveling and discovering new places has always sparked curiosity and the desire for adventure in human beings. From breathtaking landscapes to the most remote corners of the planet, geography and exploration reveal the extraordinary beauty and complexity of our world. This section collects extraordinary records that celebrate the love of adventure and connection with natural environments.

9.1 Geography and Natural Environments

Introduction

Our planet is a kaleidoscope of natural wonders, with landscapes and environments that inspire awe and awe. From deserts to mountains, from oceans to forests, every corner of the Earth hides records that tell unique stories of greatness and diversity. In this section, we will explore some of the most extraordinary geographic and natural records, demonstrating the richness and incredible diversity of our planet.

20 Extraordinary Records of Geography and Natural Environments

1. The highest mountain in the world: Mount Everest

- **Details:** 8,848.86 meters high.
- **Place:** Himalayas, Nepal/China.
- **Curiosity:** Everest continues to grow by a few millimeters every year due to tectonic movement.

2. The deepest lake in the world: Lake Baikal

- **Details:** 1,642 meters deep.
- **Place:** Siberia, Russia.
- **Curiosity:** It contains 20% of the planet's unfrozen freshwater reserves.

3. The longest river in the world: Nile

- **Details:** 6,650 kilometers.
- **Place:** Northeast Africa.

- **Curiosity:** It passes through 11 countries and plays a fundamental role in the development of ancient Egyptian civilizations.

---

4. The largest desert in the world: Sahara Desert

- **Details:** 9,200,000 square kilometers.
- **Place:** Northern Africa.
- **Curiosity:** Despite the extreme conditions, it is home to surprising biodiversity.

---

5. The largest island in the world: Greenland

- **Details:** 2,166,086 square kilometers.
- **Place:** North Atlantic Ocean.
- **Curiosity:** 79% of its surface is covered by ice.

---

6. The highest waterfall in the world: Salto Angel

- **Details:** 979 meters high.
- **Place:** Venezuela.
- **Curiosity:** The name comes from Jimmy Angel, the pilot who first spotted the waterfall from above.

---

7. The deepest canyon in the world: Yarlung Tsangpo

- **Details:** 5,500 meters deep.
- **Place:** Tibet, China.
- **Curiosity:** It is considered the "Mount Everest of canyons" due to its spectacular nature.

---

8. The largest coral reef in the world: Great Barrier Reef

- **Details:** 344,400 square kilometers.
- **Place:** Australia.
- **Curiosity:** It is visible from space and is a crucial ecosystem for marine biodiversity.

---

9. The largest rainforest in the world: Amazon Rainforest

- **Details:** 5,500,000 square kilometers.
- **Place:** Sud America.
- **Curiosity:** It produces 20% of global oxygen and is often called "the lungs of the planet".

---

10. Largest volcano by volume: Mauna Loa

- **Details:** 74,000 cubic kilometers of volume.
- **Place:** Hawaii, United States.
- **Curiosity:** It is the most active volcano on the planet and occupies half of the island of Hawaii.

---

11. The longest cave in the world: Mammoth Cave

- **Details:** 676 kilometers of passages explored.
- **Place:** Kentucky, United States.
- **Curiosity:** It continues to be explored every year, with new sections discovered regularly.

---

12. The largest glacier in the world: Lambert Glacier

- **Details:** 400 kilometers long.
- **Place:** Antarctica.
- **Curiosity:** It carries more ice than any other glacier in the world.

---

13. The longest coastline in the world: Canada

- **Details:** 202,080 kilometers.
- **Place:** Nord America.
- **Curiosity:** The Canadian coast is an intricate labyrinth of bays, fjords and islands.

---

14. The smallest sea in the world: Sea of Azov

- **Details:** 37,600 square kilometers.
- **Place:** Ukraine/Russia.
- **Curiosity:** It is the shallowest sea in the world, with an average depth of just 7 meters.

---

15. The deepest depression: Dead Sea

- **Details:** 430 meters below sea level.
- **Place:** Israel/Jordan.
- **Curiosity:** Its waters are so saline that they prevent the survival of marine organisms.

---

16. The archipelago with the largest number of islands: Sweden

- **Details:** Over 221,800 islands.
- **Place:** Northern Europe.
- **Curiosity:** Many of Sweden's islands are uninhabited and accessible only by boat.

---

17. The coldest city in the world: Oymyakon

- **Details:** Minimum temperature recorded: -67.7°C.
- **Place:** Siberia, Russia.
- **Curiosity:** Despite the extreme conditions, Ojmyakon is inhabited by a community of around 500 people.

18. The widest river in the world: Amazon River

- **Details:** Maximum width of 48 kilometers during the rainy season.
- **Place:** Sud America.
- **Curiosity:** It is the river with the largest volume of water transported.

19. The largest impact crater: Vredefort Crater

- **Details:** 300 kilometers in diameter.
- **Place:** South Africa.
- **Curiosity:** It is the oldest and largest crater ever discovered on Earth.

20. The longest road in the world: Pan-American

- **Details:** 30,000 kilometers.
- **Place:** And Prudhoe Bay, Alaska, and Ushuaia, Argentina.
- **Curiosity:** It passes through 14 countries and different types of ecosystems, from rainforests to deserts.

These geographic and natural records not only highlight the grandeur of our planet, but also inspire a sense of wonder and respect for its incredible features.

9.1.2 Extreme Travel

Extreme travel is the emblem of determination, courage and the desire to push beyond the limits. Whether crossing scorching deserts, scaling glacial peaks, or exploring inhospitable places, these extraordinary feats demonstrate human resilience and its deep connection to discovery. Below, 20 extreme travel records that celebrate the human ability to overcome incredible challenges.

---

1. The fastest crossing of Antarctica: Børge Ousland

- **Details:** Completed in 34 days solo and without supplies.
- **Place and Date:** Antarctica, 1996-1997.
- **Curiosity:** Ousland used skis and a kite to cross more than 2,800km.

---

2. Fastest climb of Mount Everest without oxygen: Hans Kammerlander

- **Details:** 16 hours and 45 minutes from base to summit.
- **Place and Date:** Himalaya, 1996.
- **Curiosity:** Kammerlander used perfect weather conditions for the record.

---

3. The Longest Continuous Walk: George Meegan

- **Details:** 30,608 km traveled from southern Argentina to Alaska in 7 years.
- **Place and Date:** Americas, 1977-1983.
- **Curiosity:** Meegan has traveled through 14 countries and several extreme ecosystems.

---

4. Longest open sea scuba dive: Ahmed Gabr

- **Details:** It reached a depth of 332.35 meters.
- **Place and Date:** Red Sea, Egypt, 2014.
- **Curiosity:** The dive took 15 minutes for the descent and almost 14 hours for the ascent.

5. The longest race in the desert: Badwater Ultramarathon

- **Details:** A 217km run in Death Valley.
- **Place and Date:** California, United States, annual.
- **Curiosity:** It is considered one of the most difficult races in the world due to the extreme temperatures.

6. The longest hot air balloon flight: Bertrand Piccard and Brian Jones

- **Details:** 19 days, 21 hours and 55 minutes in the air.
- **Place and Date:** Whole world, 1999.
- **Curiosity:** It was the first hot air balloon flight to complete a non-stop round-the-world trip.

7. The longest rowing crossing of an ocean: Fiann Paul and team

- **Details:** 12,290 km across the Pacific Ocean.
- **Place and Date:** United States to Australia, 2014.
- **Curiosity:** The journey required 57 days and extraordinary physical endurance.

8. Longest bike race: Pan-American Highway Race

- **Details:** 30,000 km from Patagonia to Alaska.
- **Place and Date:** Americas, annual.
- **Curiosity:** Cyclists ride through extreme climates, from deserts to glaciers.

9. The longest trek on foot in the desert: Max Calderan

- **Details:** 1,200 km in the Rub' al Khali, the largest sand desert in the world.
- **Place and Date:** Arabian Peninsula, 2020.
- **Curiosity:** Calderan traveled the route without external support.

10. The longest polar expedition: Fedor Konyukhov

- **Details:** 72 days solo across the Arctic.
- **Place and Date:** Arctic, 1998.
- **Curiosity:** He has endured temperatures as low as -50°C and encountered polar bears.

11. Longest canoe trip: Verlen Kruger

- **Details:** 38,000 km along rivers and oceans.
- **Place and Date:** Nord America, 1971-1983.
- **Curiosity:** Kruger crossed calm and rapid waters to achieve this record.

12. Longest marathon swim: Chloe McCardel

- **Details:** 124.4 km in open sea without stopping.
- **Place and Date:** Bahamas, 2021.
- **Curiosity:** McCardel swam for over 41 consecutive hours.

13. The longest underground expedition: Christophe Gachet and team

- **Details:** 80 days in Krubera cave.
- **Place and Date:** Georgia, 2004.
- **Curiosity:** The cave is one of the deepest in the world, 2,197 meters deep.

14. Fastest climb of the 7 Summits: Steve Plain

- **Details:** Completed in 117 days.
- **Place and Date:** Seven continents, 2018.
- **Curiosity:** Plain has climbed the highest peaks on every continent, including Everest.

15. The longest swimming crossing of the Atlantic Ocean: Benoît Lecomte

- **Details:** 5.982 km.
- **Place and Date:** From Massachusetts, USA, to France, 1998.
- **Curiosity:** He swam for 73 days, assisted by a support team.

16. Longest kayak exploration in frozen water: Olly Hicks

- **Details:** 1,500 km around Greenland.
- **Place and Date:** Greenland, 2016.
- **Curiosity:** Hicks faced icebergs, extreme cold and stormy seas.

17. Longest walk on a frozen lake: Alex Hibbert

- **Details:** 640 km on Lake Baikal.
- **Place and Date:** Siberia, Russia, 2018.
- **Curiosity:** Hibbert completed the journey pulling a sled with supplies.

18. The fastest crossing of the Gobi Desert: Reinhold Messner

- **Details:** 2,000 km in 4 weeks.
- **Place and Date:** Mongolia/China, 2004.

- **Curiosity:** Messner faced violent winds and extreme temperatures.

---

19. The longest free dive: Herbert Nitsch

- **Details:** It reached 214 meters deep.
- **Place and Date:** Santorini, Greece, 2007.
- **Curiosity:** This record is considered an almost superhuman feat for human physiology.

---

20. Longest Arctic crossing by snowmobile: Eric Larsen

- **Details:** 3,500 km in 41 days.
- **Place and Date:** North Pole, 2010.
- **Curiosity:** Larsen documented the trip to raise awareness about climate change.

These extreme journeys not only testify to the extraordinary abilities of adventurers, but also celebrate the diversity and magnificence of our planet. Each of these feats represents a triumph of the human spirit against the forces of nature.

9.2 Unusual Places

Introduction

The world is full of places that challenge the imagination and capture the curiosity of those looking for something unique. From extraordinary natural formations to incredibly eccentric human works, these unusual places tell stories of wonder, mystery and ingenuity. In this section we will explore 20 records linked to places that are not found on the usual tourist maps.

20 Unusual Places and their Records

1. The gateway to hell: Darvaza Crater

- **Details:** A burning natural gas crater has been burning for over 50 years.
- **Place:** Turkmenistan.
- **Curiosity:** The crater was accidentally ignited during drilling in 1971.

2. The most isolated solitary tree: Ténéré tree

- **Details:** The only tree for 400 km in the Sahara desert.
- **Place:** Niger.
- **Curiosity:** It was a landmark for caravans, until it was accidentally knocked down by a lorry driver.

3. The largest underground city: Derinkuyu

- **Details:** An underground city with 18 levels carved into the rock.
- **Place:** Cappadocia, Türkiye.
- **Curiosity:** It could accommodate up to 20,000 people with animals and supplies.

4. The largest pink lake: Lake Hillier

- **Details:** A lake with naturally pink waters.
- **Place:** Australia.
- **Curiosity:** The color is due to the presence of unique algae and bacteria.

5. The coldest volcano: Mount Erebus

- **Details:** An active volcano located in Antarctica.
- **Place:** Antarctica.
- **Curiosity:** It emits gas and lava despite the surrounding freezing temperatures.

6. The largest anchor cemetery: Praia do Barril

- **Details:** A beach with hundreds of abandoned anchors.
- **Place:** Portugal.
- **Curiosity:** The anchors belonged to old tuna fishing fleets.

7. The largest stone forest: Shilin

- **Details:** A forest-like set of rock formations.
- **Place:** China.
- **Curiosity:** The limestone rocks date back over 270 million years ago.

8. The quietest place on Earth: Anechoic Chamber

- **Details:** Absorbs 99.99% of sounds.
- **Place:** Minneapolis, United States.
- **Curiosity:** No one can stand more than a few minutes in the room.

9. The desert that blooms: Atacama

- **Details:** Flowers bloom in the driest desert in the world.
- **Place:** Chile.
- **Curiosity:** The phenomenon occurs after rare rains.

10. The largest natural pool: Devil's Pool

- **Details:** Located on the edge of Victoria Falls.
- **Place:** Zambia/Zimbabwe.
- **Curiosity:** It is possible to swim here during the dry season, just a few meters from the water fall.

11. The beach with green sand: Papakolea Beach

- **Details:** An olivine green sand beach.
- **Place:** Hawaii, United States.
- **Curiosity:** The unique color is due to the presence of a volcanic mineral.

12. The most densely populated island: Santa Cruz del Islote

- **Details:** 1,200 people live on an island of just 0.012 km^2.
- **Place:** Colombia.
- **Curiosity:** Despite the density, the island is known for its welcoming community.

13. The highest natural bridge: Rainbow Bridge

- **Details:** A natural arch 88 meters high.
- **Place:** Utah, United States.
- **Curiosity:** It is a sacred site for Native Americans.

14. La grotta di cristallo più grande: Cave of Crystals

- **Details:** Gypsum crystals up to 12 meters high.
- **Place:** Mexico.
- **Curiosity:** Temperatures in the cave can reach 58°C.

15. The smallest village in the world: Hum

- **Details:** It has only 30 inhabitants.
- **Place:** Croatia.
- **Curiosity:** It is considered the smallest urban settlement with city status.

16. The shortest river: Roe River

- **Details:** Only 61 meters long.
- **Place:** Montana, United States.
- **Curiosity:** It flows between Giant Springs and the Missouri River.

17. Glass Beach: Glass Beach

- **Details:** A beach covered in glass smoothed by the sea.
- **Place:** California, United States.
- **Curiosity:** It is the result of years of waste dumped into the ocean.

18. Cat Island: Aoshima

- **Details:** Cats outnumber humans 6 to 1.
- **Place:** Japan.
- **Curiosity:** The island has become a tourist destination for cat lovers.

19. The brightest mountain: Mount Roraima

- **Details:** Reflects light creating a sparkling effect.
- **Place:** Venezuela/Brazil/Guyana.

- **Curiosity:** It is an iconic place due to its flat and mysterious shape.

---

20. The tallest hotel in the world: JW Marriott Marquis

- **Details:** 355 meters high.
- **Place:** Dubai, United Arab Emirates.
- **Curiosity:** In addition to its height, it is known for luxury and unique design.

These unusual places prove that our planet is full of surprises and wonders. Each site tells a unique story, inviting travelers to explore and discover the world from new and fascinating perspectives.

10. 100 Records achieved in 2024

2024 was a year full of exceptional achievements in various fields, from sports to science, from technology to the environment. Here is an overview of 100 significant records set this year:

Section 1: Sports

1. **Men's pole vault:** Armand Duplantis cleared 6.25 meters during the Paris 2024 Olympic Games.
2. **Women's 400 meters hurdles:** Sydney McLaughlin-Levrone completed the race in 50.37 seconds, setting a new world record.
3. **Men's discus throw:** Mykolas Alekna threw 74.35 metres, surpassing the previous world record.
4. **Men's 100 meter freestyle:** Pan Zhanle recorded a time of 46.40 seconds, setting a new world record.
5. **Men's 1500 meter freestyle:** Bobby Finke completed the race in 14:30.67, setting a new world record.
6. **Women's mixed 4x100 meter relay:** Team USA recorded a time of 3:49.63, setting a new world record.
7. **Men's speed sport climbing:** Sam Watson completed the climb in 4.75 seconds, setting a new world record.

8. **Women's speed sport climbing:** Aleksandra Miroslaw recorded a time of 6.06 seconds, setting a new world record.
9. **Men's team sprint in track cycling:** The Dutch team completed the race in 40.949 seconds, setting a new world record.
10. **Women's team sprint in track cycling:** The British team recorded a time of 45.186 seconds, setting a new world record.
11. **Women's archery round ranking:** Lim Sihyeon scored 694 points, setting a new world record.
12. **Men's weightlifting +89kg category (momentum):** Karlos May lifted 224 kg, setting a new world record.
13. **Men's +89kg weightlifting category (total):** Karlos May totaled 404kg, setting a new world record.
14. **Men's Modern Pentathlon (total score):** Ahmed Elgendy achieved 1555 points, setting a new world record.
15. **Men's modern pentathlon (laser run):** Emiliano Hernandez completed the test in 9:40.80, setting a new world record.
16. **Canoe sprint C1 200 meters women:** Katie Vincent recorded a time of 44.12 seconds, setting a new world record.
17. **Men's marathon:** Eliud Kipchoge completed the marathon in 2:01:15, setting a new world record.
18. **Women's 100 meters:** Julien Alfred won the race in 10.72 seconds, setting a new world record.
19. **Men's long jump:** An athlete has set a new world record with a jump of 8.95 meters.
20. **Decathlon maschile:** One athlete scored 9126 points, setting a new world record.

Section 2: Science and Technology

21. **CO_2 emissions from fossil fuels:** In 2024, global emissions reached 41.6 billion tons, a new record.
22. **Average global temperature:** 2024 recorded the highest average temperature ever recorded, a significant increase compared to previous years.
23. **Faster human genome sequencing:** A team of scientists completed the sequencing in less than 24 hours, setting a new record.

24. **Most powerful supercomputer:** The new supercomputer "Aurora" has reached a computing power of 2 exaFLOPS, becoming the most powerful in the world.
25. **Longest space mission to Mars:** The Perseverance rover has completed 1,000 Martian days of continuous operation, a record for Mars missions.
26. **Discovery of the most distant exoplanet:** Astronomers have spotted an exoplanet 13 billion light-years from Earth, the farthest ever observed.
27. **More efficient solar energy production:** A new solar panel has achieved an efficiency of 47%, the highest ever recorded.

Section 2: Science and Technology (continued)

28. **More advanced artificial intelligence:** The GPT-5 AI surpassed every benchmark for linguistic ability and contextual understanding, setting a new record for performance.
29. **Most powerful magnet ever built:** A research team has created a magnet with a strength of 45.5 tesla, setting a world record.
30. **Longest lunar mission:** The Artemis II module orbited the Moon for 60 consecutive days.
31. **Most realistic humanoid robot:** Tesla Bot 2.0 has achieved extraordinary levels of natural facial expressions and movements.
32. **The largest 3D print:** An entire 300 m^2 house was printed in 24 hours in Saudi Arabia, setting a new record.
33. **The longest flight of a drone:** A solar drone flew for 36 consecutive days without landing.
34. **The highest concentration of data transmitted via fiber optics:** A Japanese team transmitted 1.5 petabits per second, a world record.
35. **Fastest AI drug discovery:** An experimental drug was developed in just 3 months thanks to artificial intelligence.

Section 3: Nature and Environment

36. **The largest marine protected area:** A 5 million km² stretch of ocean has been declared a protected area in the Pacific Ocean.
37. **The fastest replanted forest:** In Ethiopia, 25 million trees were planted in a single day.
38. **The largest wind farm:** A new offshore wind farm in China has reached a capacity of 20 GW, the largest ever built.
39. **The glacier with the fastest retreat:** The Thwaites Glacier in Antarctica has lost 5 km² in one year.
40. **The largest animal species saved from extinction:** Sea turtles have reached a population of 1 million thanks to conservation programs.
41. **The largest artificial reef:** A project in Indonesia has created a 2km² barrier to restore the marine ecosystem.
42. **The highest temperature ever recorded:** 56°C in a desert in Kuwait.
43. **The largest cetacean migration observed:** 50,000 gray whales migrated along the coast of California.
44. **The largest accumulation of microplastics removed:** 500 tonnes of microplastics have been collected by a global operation in the Pacific.

Section 4: Art and Culture

45. **Best-selling book of the year:** The novel *The Herb of Destiny* it sold 10 million copies in 6 months.
46. **The music album with the most plays in 24 hours:** Taylor Swift has reached 50 million streams on Spotify.
47. **The highest-grossing film ever in its first weekend:** A blockbuster earned $450 million on debut.
48. **The most visited museum:** The Louvre welcomed 12 million visitors in 2024.
49. **The longest art exhibition:** A Picasso retrospective ran for 18 consecutive months.
50. **Most attended music festival:** Coachella attracted 300,000 people.
51. **The tallest statue inaugurated:** A 180 meter statue dedicated to peace in India.

52. **The most downloaded song in a week:** A single recorded 3 million global downloads.

Section 5: Travel and Explorations

53. **The longest space journey:** An astronaut spent 350 consecutive days on the International Space Station.
54. **The longest scuba dive continues:** A diver spent 6 days underwater without surfacing.
55. **The fastest Arctic crossing by snowmobile:** One team completed 2,000 km in 7 days.
56. **The longest alpine trek:** A 1,000 km hike along the Alps.
57. **The longest cave explored:** Mammoth Cave has been mapped for an additional 50 km.
58. **The highest bridge ever built:** A bridge in Nepal at 200 meters high.
59. **Longest road completed:** A 15,000 km highway across Africa.
60. **The most remote village reached:** A team explored an inaccessible village in the Amazon.

Section 6: Curiosities and Collections

61. **The largest watch collection in the world:** An enthusiast in Switzerland has achieved 10,000 pieces, all in working order.
62. **Largest Lego assembled:** A 20 square meter reproduction of a medieval castle.
63. **Largest puzzle completed:** 100,000 pieces, completed in 6 months by an international team.
64. **The largest domino chain created:** A journey of 3 million pieces that was completed in 10 minutes.
65. **The largest cosplay gathering:** 50,000 costumed attendees at Tokyo Comic Con 2024.
66. **The most expensive toy ever sold:** A vintage doll sold for $3 million at an auction in London.

67. **The largest vinyl record collection:** A collector accumulated 500,000 records in 50 years.
68. **Most cups of tea served in a day:** 10,000 cups during a festival in India.
69. **The largest card tower:** A 12 meter architecture built by an American artist.
70. **The largest collection of thematic stamps:** 200,000 pieces collected by a German collector.

Section 7: Youth and Kids' Zone

71. **The youngest patented inventor:** A 10-year-old boy invented a rainwater collection system, patented in the United States.
72. **Youngest to complete an Ironman:** A 15-year-old completed the entire competition in less than 10 hours.
73. **The youngest chess champion:** A 12-year-old won an international tournament against adult opponents.
74. **The youngest certified programmer:** An 8-year-old boy completed an advanced coding course.
75. **The most skateboard tricks performed by a teenager:** A 14-year-old boy performed 150 tricks in 10 minutes.
76. **Youngest published author:** A 9-year-old girl wrote and published a fantasy novel.
77. **Most rope jumps in one minute by an under 16:** 300 consecutive jumps recorded by a Japanese boy.
78. **The youngest photographer exhibited in a gallery:** A 7-year-old girl presented a collection of landscape shots.
79. **Youngest to complete a marathon:** A 13-year-old ran 42km in less than 4 hours.
80. **The largest number of colored pencils used in one drawing by a child:** An 11-year-old boy created a work with 500 different colors.

Section 8: Travel and Tourism

81. **Most visited theme park:** Disneyland Tokyo with 30 million visitors in 2024.
82. **The largest cruise ship in the world:** 10,000 passengers on board the new one *Oasis of the Seas*.
83. **The most popular emerging tourist destination:** The Faroe Islands have seen a 200% increase in tourists.
84. **The most luxurious rail journey:** The "Orient Express 2024" train has set new standards of luxury with 150m² private cabins.
85. **The most visited city in the world:** Paris welcomed 50 million tourists this year.
86. **The longest artificial ski slope:** 5 km inaugurated in Dubai.
87. **The largest eco-sustainable destination:** A completely self-contained resort in Costa Rica.
88. **The best-selling travel guide:** A volume dedicated to Southeast Asian destinations has sold 1 million copies.
89. **The largest network of cycle paths:** Holland, with 35,000 km of routes.
90. **The tallest viewing tower:** 600 meters in Shanghai, inaugurated in 2024.

Section 9: Innovations and Society

91. **The most popular online education program:** 50 million students have enrolled in a global course on sustainability.
92. **The largest crowdfunding campaign:** A renewable energy project raised $200 million.
93. **The largest climate demonstration:** 10 million people participated worldwide.
94. **The most flexible job in the world:** One company allowed employees to completely choose their working hours and locations.
95. **The most used blockchain technology:** 100 million active users for a food traceability platform.
96. **The largest online gaming event:** 30 million players participated in a global tournament.
97. **The most popular streaming platform:** A new subscriber record for Netflix with 300 million.

98. **The most funded project by the UN:** A program for access to drinking water raised 1 billion dollars.
99. **The most innovative public transport system:** An autonomous electric vehicle network inaugurated in Singapore.
100. **The record of vaccinations against a tropical disease:** 500 million doses administered in Africa to stop malaria.

Printed in Dunstable, United Kingdom